LIFE'S
Compass
FOR ETERNAL
TREASURE

3rd Edition

STUDY GUIDE INCLUDED

Sarah Malanowski

Life's Compass for Eternal Treasure
Copyright © 2007, 2014, 2018 by Sarah Malanowski. All rights reserved.
Published by The Priceless Journey

No part of this publication may be reproduced, stored in a retrieval system or transmitted in any way by any means, electronic, mechanical, photocopy, recording or otherwise without the prior permission of the author except as provided by USA copyright law.

Scripture quotations marked (NIV) are taken from the Holy Bible, New International Version®, Copyright © 1973, 1978, 1984 by International Bible Society. Used by permission of Zondervan Publishing House. All rights reserved. All scripture verses mentioned in this book are NIV unless otherwise noted.

Scripture quotations marked (AMP) are taken from the Amplified Bible, Copyright © 1954, 1958, 1962, 1964, 1965, 1987 by The Lockman Foundation. Used by permission.

Scripture quotations marked (ESV) are from The Holy Bible, English Standard Version. Copyright © 2001 by Crossway Bibles, a publishing ministry of Good News Publishers. Used by permission. All rights reserved.

All Scripture passages are from The Message Bible (MSG) unless otherwise stated. Copyright © 1994, 1995, 1996, 2000, 2001, 2002. Used by permission of NavPress Publishing Group.

Scripture quotations marked (NASB) are taken from the New American Standard Bible, Copyright © 1960, 1962, 1963, 1968, 1971, 1972, 1973, 1975, 1977, 1995 by the Lockman Foundation. Used by permission. All rights reserved.

Scripture quotations marked (NKJV) are taken from the New King James Version. Copyright © 1982 by Thomas Nelson, Inc. Used by permission. All rights reserved.

Printed in United States of America

ISBN: 978-1-947066-16-8

1. Spiritual Growth
2. Family
3. Inspiration

Cover & Book Design by Sondra Howe

What Others Are Saying

"Some people take great delight in making the simple complex. In Life's Compass for Eternal Treasure, Sarah Malanowski does just the opposite. She brings the complex and sublime into the simple realm of possibility. This book awakens faith and strengthens our trust in a God who loves us. Jesus is lifted up and His Spirit will touch every reader in a deep, deep way."

— Dr. Ron Walborn
Dean of Alliance Theological Seminary Nyack College

"It has been my extreme privilege to preview Sarah's book and experience her journey to know God more deeply and intimately. From beginning to end you will be blessed by her honesty, transparency, and obedient devotion to God and His Word. Prepare to learn and grow spiritually."

— Kathleen Turner
Educator
Vista, California

"As I was reading I kept thinking that some very sophisticated ideas were presented in a very accessible fashion. It is that accessibility that allowed the Word of God to penetrate my heart and provide for me inspiration for my journey."

— Pastor Mark Bjorlo
The Journey North Community Church, Brainerd, Minnesota

Dedication

I praise and thank the Author of my life story. God gave me these verses as a young girl to guide me and keep me ever going in His direction. It is a privilege to write about His work and His continued faithfulness in my life.

Matthew 6:21

FOR WHERE YOUR TREASURE IS, THERE WILL YOUR HEART BE ALSO

Contents

SECTION ONE | TRUST

Chapter 1	Who Needs Blueprints?	13
Chapter 2	He said, "GO!"	19
Chapter 3	No Need for Extravagance	27
Chapter 4	Timing is Everything	33
Chapter 5	Friends...Just the Right People at Just the Right Time	39
Chapter 6	Victory in the Battles	45

SECTION TWO | DELIGHT

Chapter 7	Daddy, Daddy	51
Chapter 8	Time is Not Ours	59
Chapter 9	Refocusing the View	65
Chapter 10	Living the Life	71
Chapter 11	An Eagle's Flight	77

SECTION THREE | COMMIT

Chapter 12	Finding True North	85
Chapter 13	Plan of Action	91
Chapter 14	Let 's Talk	97
Chapter 15	Letting God Speak	105
Chapter 16	Stretch Those Legs	115

SECTION FOUR | RIGHTEOUSNESS

Chapter 17	Wearing the Right Shoe	123
Chapter 18	A Walk through the Woods	129
Chapter 19	Delightful Value	135
Chapter 20	Call to Commitment	143
Chapter 21	A Fresh Start	149

STUDY GUIDE — 155

Foreword

Life's Compass! What is a compass? What is its purpose? The big Webster dictionary says: *compass—an instrument for determining direction; a magnetic compass points to the magnetic north.*

Today because of modern technology, we have the privilege of possessing an instrument far more sophisticated than the old-time Boy Scout pocket compass. What explorer, or everyday traveler, would even begin a journey through an unknown landscape without a compass or some type of GPS device that would provide a dependable standard to determine the correct direction?

I was recently asked to speak at a small church in Gainesville, 100 miles north of my home in Spring Hill, Florida. Even though I had the address, I had no idea where it was located. So, imagine how foolish it would have been for me to get on I-75, and head north, and hope I could "*feel*" my way to the intended destination. However, when I entered the address into my *smart* phone, my authentic standard, *she* took me directly to the site, and even by the fastest route.

Life's Compass: How and where do we gain the direction for **life**? By and large, it comes as a way of life, from home, family, friends and relatives. There are also our life-experiences, direction, learning from the neighborhood we are raised in, book-learning from the schools we attend, and lessons we learn from fellow students we hang out with.

Practical Question: Do any, or all of these life-learning sources provide us an authentic standard by which we are guaranteed to reach our intended destination... our desired life goals? In light of this critical question, think for a moment about the meaning embedded in these Bible verses.

> *The heart is deceitful above all things, and desperately sick;*

who can understand it? Jeremiah 17:9

*There is a way that seems right to a man,
but its end is the way to death.* Proverbs 14:12

*The god of this world has blinded the minds of unbelievers,
to keep them from seeing the gospel of Christ.*
2 Corinthians 4:4 (ESV)

Knowing the cultural teaching of our day, do you feel totally confident in the direction your life has taken, if absorbed by default from family, friends, neighbors, classmates, TV cultural standards, and teachers or bosses? The book you are holding in your hand will give you practical, dependable, accurate, authentic directions to the life God has designed for you to live and enjoy.

Think of the meaning of this verse, right in the center of the Psalm passage that Sarah builds her book around:

*Delight yourself in God alone, and He will give you
the desires of your heart.* Psalm 37:4

The premise of the book is that we will never achieve the *true-north* desires of our heart, if we do not allow God to direct our lives.

*There is a way that **seems** to be right* ... but if we have chosen by "*feeling*," without God, how tragic it would be to get *there* and realize "I wish I had never done that!" The deepest desires of our heart, at any given time, may never come close to the adventures and outcomes God has designed for our life ... because *the heart is deceitful*.

God's desires for us will be far more fulfilling than we could ever imagine for ourselves. Of course, this is the exact opposite of what social media and today's culture will push on you, because their standard for course direction is totally self-centered and self-indulgent, rather than focused on the magnetic spiritual north of God's ways.

In *Life's Compass for Eternal Treasure*, Sarah slowly walks us through the Psalm 37 passage, phrase by phrase, unfolding practical spiritual truths. She then illustrates the application of these spiritual principles with stories from her own life.

If you *know* Sarah, you will see and feel her kind caring personality in the stories she shares – like walking through the woods holding the hand of a 10-year old New York City boy who has never seen so many trees and rocks. The truth revealed is excellent. If you have *never met* Sarah, you will sense her deep genuine love for Jesus and passion to become more and more like Him. Her passion will draw you through the book, creating a desire to know Him in a maturing personal way.

Over and over, with practical Bible verses, Sarah illustrates how God's way is always best. And that makes common sense, when you understand that God loves you supremely and unconditionally . . . more than anyone else ever has or could!

I encourage you to read through this book as I did, not as a speed-reading endeavor, but prayerfully and thoughtfully, asking the Spirit of God to bring His truth to light in your heart and life experiences. You see, He loves you, right where you are. And He loves you so much, that He desires to guide you step by step and day by day on a life course, so that you may experience His love, acceptance and fulfillment. Then you will know His peace, His joy and His blessing.

Chaplain David Pletincks
Retired Pastor of Christian & Missionary Alliance
Chaplain of The Priceless Journey

Introduction

Throughout my life there has been one passage of scripture that continues to stand out. No matter what life throws my way, I can continue to go back to this simple passage. It states the importance of trusting God, delighting in God, and committing my way to Him. Then it tells me the outcome when I follow these three simple truths. Nothing lays down a stronger foundation for me than the words emphasized in this passage. I found in them not just simple words, but a path to follow. This passage directs me to the Father's heart, a place that I so often need to go. This may be a small portion of scripture with simple truths, but it has a big message with lasting effects.

> Psalm 37:3–6 reads, **"Trust in the Lord and do good; dwell in the land and enjoy safe pasture. Delight yourself in the Lord and He will give you the desires of your heart. Commit your way to the Lord; trust in Him and He will do this: He will make your righteousness shine like the dawn, the justice of your cause like the noonday sun."**

Trust. Some see that word and immediately avert their eyes. Trust, what do you mean? Don't you know where I've been? I've been hurt by those closest to me … my scars are deep, my pain is indescribable. I can't trust. Delight … sure, I can do that. That's easier than trusting, but it's not how God begins this passage. He wants us to trust in Him before we do anything else. So let's explore this. What does trust mean? How do we get there? With what do we need to trust God? Is it possible to trust Him? Will He fail me like so many others have done?

All of these questions and many more will be answered in the coming chapters. I invite you to come on an adventure with me. Let's discover the heart of God together and learn how to move to the rhythm of His heartbeat for us.

In God's Grip of Grace,

Sarah

The purpose of Christianity is not to avoid difficulty, but to produce a character adequate to meet it when it comes. It does not make life easy; rather it tries to make us great enough for life.

—James L. Christensen

Chapter 1
WHO NEEDS BLUEPRINTS?

Webster's dictionary says the first definition of trust is "Total confidence in the integrity, ability, and good character of another." Wow! What a loaded definition, and this is only the beginning. Is God worthy of our total confidence? The answer is not complicated by any means. Yes, God is absolutely worthy of our total confidence. History has shown over and over again that

Some trust in chariots and some in horses, but we trust in the name of the Lord our God.
— Psalm 20:7

God is faithful to His people. He will not let us down. All too often we become like the Israelites who totally trusted God when He was performing the miraculous but lost sight of Him when things got a little rough. Did God change? By no means, He was the same! The Bible says, "Jesus Christ is the same yesterday and today and forever" (Hebrews 13:8). Who changes? We do! I change! Yes, sometimes the seas tend to get a little rough, but God remains in the boat with us at all times.

Let's look at the story of the disciples and their little ride with Jesus through a storm. In Luke 8:22–25, we see Jesus directing His disciples to get into a boat and sail across the lake. He gave simple instructions:

TRUST

"Let's go over to the other side of the lake." They got in the boat and started heading to the other side, but on their way a storm arose. The disciples were shaken by this sudden storm. They saw it as an obstacle standing in the way of their goal. They simply wanted to get to the other side and the storm was preventing them from doing so. Or was it really preventing them? Did they miss out on an adventure? Jesus was in the boat with them. However, He was sleeping through the storm. He was not bothered by the winds or the waves. There is a great reason for this.

The disciples only saw danger through their human eyes. They did not see the greater good in this, which was an adventure with the Son of God. They woke Jesus up in their pure madness because they feared drowning. Jesus awoke and rebuked the wind and the raging waters. At His simple rebuke, all became calm once again. He turned to His disciples and said, "Where is your faith?" In other words, don't you trust Me? Don't you trust that I want the best for you and I will take care of you through every storm?

Now faith is being sure of what we hope for and certain of what we do not see.
— Hebrews 11:1

All too often we look at the wind and the waves and yell for God to wakeup, because we are fearful of drowning. God does not have intentions of letting us drown. He is in the boat, and His purpose for us is to stretch our faith that we may come to trust Him even just a little more. Trust is total confidence in the one who made us. It is complete surrender to the one who has planned greater good for us since the beginning.

Can you think of any areas of life in which people put their total undeserving confidence? I certainly can! I think about bridges and the human hands that put them together. Man is full of flaws, yet he is used over and over again to create flawless structures. There is no room for error in the design of a bridge. One error could mean many lives lost. Yet, I have crossed over them many times in my life without thinking about their possible faults.

I've never stopped at the beginning of the bridge and said, "Can someone show me the blueprints for this bridge? I can't drive across it until I see them." That would be ridiculous. Sure, I could look at the blueprints, but they wouldn't mean much to me. So then why is it that we often ask God for the blueprints of our life when He is a flawless Creator? His design is immaculate.

Another area that we put total trust in is vehicles used for transportation. Some examples are trucks, boats, trains, buses, and airplanes. You name it, and we put our confidence in it. Do we put our confidence in these things because of the great warranty offered with them? The last time I took a bus, no one provided me with a warranty that said I would make it to my destination in one piece.

I've never been to an assembly line to see how my vehicle was put together, yet I totally depend on it to get me from point A to point B. All too often God uses vehicles of circumstance to draw me closer to Him. I don't get to see why it's there or how it got there.

I don't even get to choose how it looks. In this circumstance I find myself needing to put my full confidence in God, letting Him direct my steps and making me into a greater person through perseverance. This is one of the vehicles God uses. Other vehicles you might know of are faith, patience, long suffering, and joy. Do these sound familiar? If so, it's because they are part of the fruit of the spirit. We attain the likeness of God's Son by grabbing hold of the ways He wants to produce character in us, and many times this character is produced through long standing in His presence.

TRUST

I am learning on a daily basis that I need to trust God with every detail of my life. There have been many times in my life where I've wondered what God is doing, because the circumstances I see don't fit in my picture perfect world. Then God reminds me that the race is not over, and I'm still running for Him. And sometimes there will be hills to climb, valleys to drudge through, and deserts without water to quench my thirst. These times are used to further my growth in God.

Blessed is the man who perseveres under trial, because when he has stood the test, he will receive the crown of life that God has promised to those who love him.

— James 1:12

In fact, I have gone through some things in life that I might not have chosen for myself, but each one has taught me a valuable lesson that I really couldn't live without. In this I have learned not to live in regret, but to see everything as a vehicle of learning. The vehicles aren't too pleasant to ride in at times, but the destination is always worth the drive. So in which areas of our lives do we need to trust God? The answer is every area. We need to trust God with our finances, our family, our future, our relationships with others, and our desires. This is only naming a few. I can tell you that God has stretched me in all of these areas. Many times I have wondered where the provision will come for bills that are waiting to be paid. I ask, "Lord, can't you just grow a money tree in my backyard?" This is my unending question. Wouldn't life be simpler if there were such a seed to grow a tree like this? No, not at all! My faith in God would not be as strong as it is, if I could just walk to my backyard and get money every time I needed it.

Instead, God grips my heart over and over again by taking me down the road of supply and demand. I know my part, I have my requests, and He has the supply. He's not a bank to run to like some may think. It's not like the game Monopoly, where you get $200 every time you pass Go. He is not a miser who holds back or keeps everything from us. His name is not Scrooge. He is Jehovah Jireh, my provider! Your provider! He is in control of all that can be provided when needed. He does not hold anything back from us. He has given even His own Son, who is worth more than any financial need.

All that I have seen teaches me to trust the Creator for all I have not seen.

—Ralph Waldo Emerson

Chapter 2
HE SAID, "GO!"

One area in which we need to trust God is the means by which He provides for us. There are so many things in life that really don't make sense at all. No matter how you seem to put the puzzle together, there's always one piece missing. I know, because I have tried to put the puzzle of my life together many times and God continues to remind me that He's the One responsible for all the pieces. Resting in Him and watching His hand go to work is a much better place to be than trying to put the puzzle together myself.

And my God will liberally supply (fill to the full) your every need according to His riches in glory in Christ Jesus. (AMPC)
— Philippians 4:19

One great example I have of when God provided for my needs was when I was getting ready to go to college. Through some unfortunate events, my bank account was completely depleted of funds. This occurred only a few weeks before I was supposed to leave for college. I had a choice to make. I could stay home and raise money to go for the following year, or I could simply go and trust that God would provide my every need. Well, I chose to stay home. I unpacked every single box. I canceled my plane ticket. Everything I had done to prepare to go

TRUST

to college I simply undid. I thought this was the best solution; the only logical solution. Thankfully, God had other plans.

I had made my decision to stay home on a Thursday. Sunday morning I did not feel like worshiping because I could not understand why God would have me stay when everything in my heart told me I was ready to go to school in New York. Right there in my seat at church God met me. He whispered in my ear, "Go."

I thought, go where?

I heard it again, only a little more defined . . . "Go!" Again, I thought, go where?

One last time, I felt God say, "Go to New York!"

I simply chuckled to myself thinking, yeah, right! Have you seen my bank account? I have nothing.

...being confident of this that he who began a good work in you will carry it on to completion until the day of Christ Jesus.
— Philippians 1:6

God continued to whisper in my ear the sweet word I needed to hear, "GO!"

His voice resonated in my ear like a cymbal that had just been sounded. The strings of my heart were played and my mind was stirring with possibilities. Again, I was down to two choices: listen to God and go by faith that He would provide or stay at home and ignore the call He had on my life.

My initial response was to simply ignore the call. That seemed like a much easier thing to do, so I walked away that day thinking, *There's no*

TRUST

way I'm going to college. On Monday morning I called my admissions counselor to let her know that I would not be able to attend school this year. She asked if it was due to financial strain. I said yes. She said she wanted to check into some grants and scholarships to see if there was more money they could give me to come. My heart leaped with joy at the thought of going where I knew God had called me to go, but my mind was thinking otherwise.

Before I got off the phone with her, she let me know that she would be calling me by the end of the day. I went for a long walk, expressing to God everything that was on my heart. I spent time apologizing for not trusting Him and for not walking by faith. I let Him know that I wanted my steps to be determined by Him. Just like the Word says, "In his heart a man plans his course, but the Lord determines his steps" (Proverbs 16:9). Yes, that's what I wanted. I want my steps to be ordered by God. He simply said the same thing He said to me Sunday morning, "GO!" I said okay this time, knowing that He must have a great plan that I couldn't possibly understand.

Later, I received a phone call from Nyack College letting me know that they would be able to support me with another scholarship. They asked if this was enough to get me to come, and I said yes. So again I packed my boxes, I bought

For we walk by faith, not by sight.
— 2 Corinthians 5:7 (NASB)

my plane ticket, and I was off. I had no idea what God had in store for me. All I knew was that I was supposed to go. I stepped on an airplane about two weeks later with not even a single penny to my name. I was going to New York by complete faith.

That first year of college stretched me beyond belief. I wasn't able to find a job until about a month into my freshman year, but that job lasted me throughout my whole college career. I was blessed to work in an environment where people cared about my well-being and decided that they wanted to employ me throughout my college experience. Did this happen by chance? Absolutely not! God had all of this in mind before I even came to be a thought in my parents' minds. He knew He would make a way for me to get through college, and He did what no one else was capable of doing. He walked me through my college years, providing for every semester and every book to study.

Horatio G. Spafford was a good example of a man in history who trusted in God despite his gloomy circumstances. Many of you may not recognize his name, but the song that he wrote might be familiar to you. He wrote the hymn "It Is Well with My Soul." The title of this song and its words describe a complete opposite picture than would be described by Spafford's life. The story behind this hymn only enriches its meaning.

This hymn was written after two major traumas in Spafford's life. The first trauma to devastate his life was the Chicago Fire of October 1871, which destroyed him financially. Shortly after, while crossing the Atlantic, all four of Spafford's daughters died in a collision with another ship. Spafford's wife, Anna survived and sent him the now famous telegram, "Saved alone." Several weeks later, as Spafford's own ship passed near the spot where his daughters died, the Holy Spirit inspired these words. They speak to an eternal hope in believers, no matter the circumstances they face in life.

I encourage you to imagine yourself in Spafford's shoes and let the words of this song be a sweet balm for your many wounds. May you find healing in these words, just as Spafford did when they rang so sweetly in his ears. Here are the words expressed from Spafford's soul.

TRUST

It Is Well With My Soul

When peace, like a river, attendeth my way,
When sorrows like sea billows roll;
Whatever my lot, Thou has taught me to say,
It is well; it is well, with my soul.
It is well, with my soul,
It is well, with my soul,
It is well; it is well, with my soul.
Though Satan should buffet, though trial should come,
Let this blest assurance control,
That Christ has regarded my helpless estate,
And hath shed His own blood for my soul.
It is well, with my soul,
It is well, with my soul,
It is well; it is well, with my soul.

My sin, oh, the bliss of this glorious thought!
My sin, not in part, but the whole,
Is nailed to the cross, and I bear it no more,
Praise the Lord, praise the Lord, O my soul!
It is well, with my soul,
It is well, with my soul,
It is well; it is well, with my soul.

And Lord, haste the day when my faith shall be sight,
The clouds be rolled back as a scroll;
The trump shall resound, and the Lord shall descend,
Even so, it is well with my soul.
It is well, with my soul,
It is well, with my soul,
It is well; it is well, with my soul.

TRUST

The next time you feel beat up by the storms that surround you, think of the words of this song and trust that "It is well, with your soul..."

"For you created my inmost being; you knit me together in my mother's womb. I praise you because I am fearfully and wonderfully made; your works are wonderful, I know that full well. My frame was not hidden from you when I was made in the secret place. When I was woven together in the depths of the earth, your eyes saw my unformed body. All the days ordained for me were written in your book before one of them came to be."

(Psalm 139:13–16)

This passage of scripture expresses the immensity of the time God takes to determine each part of who we are. One thing that amazes me over and over again is the design of the stars in the sky. They are too numerous for you or me to count, but still God took the time to set each one in its place. Genesis 1:16–17 says, "He also made the stars. God set them in the expanse of the sky to give light on the earth." Can you imagine taking time to set each individual star in place? I certainly can't, but God did it. And He continues to do it each day in us. He sets every event in place for us and knows the details. He hasn't overlooked anything in you. Quite the opposite is true. He has taken the time to make sure every detail of your life falls into place like it needs to. I'm not meaning the way we would like it to be done but just the way God knows is best.

I love referring to this passage of scripture when people ask me how God has provided for me. Just as I can't fathom what God was thinking when He placed every star in the heavens, I also don't know why He provides financially for me the way He does. A pattern for this does not seem to exist, at least not one I can make out. If I had things my way, the money would always be there when I think I need it. I'd never

TRUST

have to worry about where it was coming from. Sure, that sounds great, but my faith would never grow. I have seen God provide me with cars, computers, kitchen supplies, rocking chairs, beds, furniture, and numerous other things. I've watched His hand move to supply all my needs.

Now remember what the scripture says about this. "And my God will meet all your needs according to His glorious riches in Christ Jesus" (Philippians 4:19). The Life Application Bible has a great note to go along with this. It says,

> ***We can trust that God will always meet our needs. Whatever we need on earth He will always supply ... We must remember, however, the difference between our wants and our needs. Most people want to feel good and avoid discomfort or pain. We may not get all that we want. By trusting in Christ, our attitudes and appetites can change from wanting everything to accepting His provision and power to live for Him.***

Trusting God with the details means letting Him take over even those areas in our lives that we want to hoard for ourselves. It's tough sometimes to hand over the reins, but God has a much better ride in store for us as His children. God wants to do amazing things in your life. Allow Him to do so by simply saying yes to His plan for you and letting go of your mistrust in Him or of Him. Your adventure with God can only begin from here, when you let Him lead.

As a boy I toted two buckets of water, one balancing the other, grace works the same way. People see our 'Bucket of Troubles' easy enough. What they don't see is the 'Bucket of Grace' that balances out the 'Bucket of Troubles.'

—Joe Pursiful

Chapter 3
NO NEED FOR EXTRAVAGANCE

Another area in which we need to trust God is our families. This is a very difficult area to hand over to God. There was one point in my life where everything seemed to go wrong at the same time. My grandpa was going to have a quadruple bypass heart surgery, as well as my uncle. My grandma found out that she had cancer, and my mother was going through some of her own physical ailments. This all happened in such a short period of time that my mind was overwhelmed by the weight of it on a daily basis. I kept asking why God would give me so much to handle.

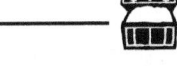

Again, I found myself going for a walk to talk to God and ask for answers. I truly was at my wit's end, wondering what I could do to somehow make things better with all of the circumstances

Cast your burden upon the Lord and He will sustain you; He will never allow the righteous to be shaken.
— Psalm 55:22 (*NASB*)

that were going awry in my life. While I was walking, I heard a small whimper. I looked around but saw nothing. So I continued to walk. The whimper became stronger with each step I took, so I looked again. The sound of this whimper was coming from some branches on the side of the trail. I looked all throughout the bushes to try and find the source of this cry. This cry was coming from a small bird stuck in the branches.

TRUST

I carefully bent down to withdraw the bird from the branches then gently held it in my hands.

I walked the bird back to a place on the grass where I could simply pray for it. I prayed that the Lord would heal his broken body and enable him to fly. Now this might seem like a simple prayer to some, but I knew God wanted to teach me something through this bird. So I prayed my heart out for him. While I was praying, I felt a rubbing against my hand. I looked to see what was happening. The bird was rubbing its head against my hand, and as it did so a scale came off of its eye. The bird then flew away.

It was as simple as that. No extravagant prayer. No doctor. No medicine. It was just a plea to God for this little bird that was hiding in my hand. God showed me through this little bird that I somehow had gotten a scale over my own eye. This slowly occurred while I was trusting in my own means to get by instead of God's authority to break through every situation.

Deuteronomy 33:25 says, "The bolts of your gates will be iron and bronze, and your strength will equal your days." God will give us strength to equal our days. The task is never too big for Him and the method of meeting our needs is simple when compared to His greatness.

It's so easy to get overwhelmed by the circumstances of life when that is all we look at. Everything in each family situation turned out fine. God knew what He was doing. There was no reason for me to worry about it.

As the heavens are higher than the earth, so are my ways higher than your ways and my thoughts than your thoughts.

— Isaiah 55:9

TRUST

In the book, *The Attributes of God* by A. W. Tozer, I have found some simple truths to guide me in seeing God in the complexity of His thought. Tozer talks about a place in Pennsylvania near where he lived. He describes it as a beautiful place where you can see sun-kissed hills and mystic blues in the setting of the sun. He also talks about creeks that run into rivers and on to the sea. He describes it in such a fond way.

One day, he went back to visit this beautiful place that he had remembered, and it no longer had that beautiful feel. Instead, it was a barren place with nothing of beauty to offer. He talks about his grief in walking away from a place that he once knew to be so amazing. Sometimes in our lives, beautiful things can be happening, but bulldozers come out of nowhere to destroy the pretty scenery in which we live. I know that all too often I have been shaken by the things that surround my family atmosphere. I found myself often worrying about my family members when I was away from them.

At one point, I remember my brother being in a treatment center, and all I could think was *why*? Why God? Why does he have to go through this? Isn't there something I can do to take his place? I sat near a pond and just cried my eyes out at the loss I was feeling for my brother. God met me where I was and reminded me that it was His responsibility to take care of my family. He knows the hairs on their heads, and He knows how to best love them.

At the time things looked grim, and I thought my brother would never leave the treatment center. He was so stubborn, but God saw through it all. God didn't let him stay where he was. It was only for a season. You could say a bulldozer definitely did an overhaul in his life, but now he is an amazing young man who I can only begin to describe as a world changer.

TRUST

The ugly gash in nature that Tozer describes in his book doesn't remain this way. In fact, it changed drastically. He says,

> *I went back in a few more years, and do you know what nature had done? Dear old busy, enthusiastic, fun-loving, joyous Mother Nature began to draw a green veil over that ugly gash. And now if you go back you will see it has cured itself. It's God Almighty in that!*

There are often pitfalls in life. For me, I've seen many of these pitfalls happen within my family environment. I have had to entrust them to God and know that He is responsible for their every need. I remember my dad telling me that he didn't worry about me because He knew I was on loan from God … I was God's daughter to take care of. In fact, he told me the story of when he let go of all of his kids, knowing that only God can determine our steps.

Back when I was nine years old, a fire took my family home from us. We lost everything! Well, I shouldn't say everything. We did walk away with our lives and a sense that God loved us enough to spare us from what could have been even more of a tragedy. My dad was on a fishing trip in Canada. When he came back it was to a terrible surprise.

The house was all burned, so we left one of the burnt couches in the front yard with a big ole sign on it that said, "We're okay! We're at the neighbor's house!" Dad told me in that moment, he realized that God had His hand on our lives and ultimately God was responsible for us. I have come to learn that my responsibility for my family does not override God's love

So do not fear, for I am with you; do not be dismayed, for I am your God. I will strengthen you and help you; I will uphold you with my righteous right hand.

— Isaiah 41:10

TRUST

for them. He is the one who takes intimate time with them and shows them of His love. I'm simply here to be a daughter and a sister. That's an easier job to handle.

Do you think you can entrust your family to God? Do you know that He already knows the steps that they will take? He is guiding them. I watched three of my siblings walk down a very terrible road, and through it my heart was broken. But God saw them for what they would be in Him and how these circumstances would mold their character. We are God's, simply on loan to our families. We need to keep in perspective that only God can make each day count.

There is a time for everything, and a season for every activity under Heaven.

—Ecclesiastes 3:1

Chapter 4
TIMING IS EVERYTHING

We also need to trust God with the future. Look at the story of Abraham. Genesis 12 starts an unbelievable journey for Abraham—then known as Abram. The Lord had said to Abram,

Leave your country, your people and your father's household and go to the land I will show you. I will make you into a great nation and I will bless you; I will make your name great, and you will be a blessing. I will bless those who bless you, and whoever curses you I will curse; and all people on earth will be blessed through you. (Genesis 12:1–3)

God simply said, "Leave!" He did not tell Abram the future country to go to. He did not say how they would get there or by what means they would have to secure their way. He simply said "Go!" Then He proceeded to share with Abram a very specific blessing. The

By faith Abraham, when called to go to a place he would later receive as his inheritance, obeyed and went, even though he did not know where he was going.
— Hebrews 11:8

blessing was greater than any man would ever hear, yet Abram had no idea how it would be accomplished. I love his response to God. Genesis 12:4 says, "So Abram left, as the Lord had told him …" He did not leave room for questions, nor did he sit and wonder where he would end up. He simply followed God's instructions.

Trust. Yes, I would say this is one of the greatest responses in trust that I have ever come to know. Abram followed God even when it did not make sense to leave home and everything he knew. We too need to entrust our future to God. We need to let Him determine each step.

This story continues in great detail and God truly shows Himself to be faithful to Abram. In Genesis 17:5–6 God shows up to add another piece of the puzzle to Abram's life. God says, "No longer will you be called Abram; your name will be Abraham, for I have made you a father of many nations. I will make you very fruitful; I will make nations of you, and kings will come from you." Throughout chapter seventeen, God continues to make a covenant with Abraham. This covenant reveals the intimacy of our God who ordains every moment and follows through on every promise. It is so very important to follow His dreams and desires for our lives.

I had a situation like this arise in my life. Just a little over three years ago, I felt God was asking me to move. At the time I was living in Delaware working at a very nice job. I had friends and family galore. Life was good! There were no complaints from me, but out of nowhere God simply said, "It's time to go!" This time God was asking me to return home. I fought with Him for about three months, letting Him know that it just didn't make sense to return home after everything that I had established in Delaware. I asked Him if He was paying attention and if He could see how good things were going for me. None of that mattered. He simply was asking me to return home.

Yes, my situation was a little different than Abraham's because I was returning home, not leaving home. Well, in one sense anyway. Yes, I did grow up in Minnesota, but my home was now in Delaware. God

TRUST

had surrounded me with so many great people that I was unwilling to leave them behind. Thankfully, God doesn't take no as an answer. I would be in trouble if He did, as He knows so much better than I do what is best for my life.

Through the next three months, God proceeded to show me in many ways that it was time to return home. He sent people along my path to encourage me and let me know that this was the time of my life to make changes. He sent people to quote verses from the Bible that plainly gave direction towards home. He also gave me a dream, a dream that I will never forget.

In the dream, I was walking towards a huge oak tree and standing at the foot of the oak tree was Jesus. I saw Him beckon me and ask me to come closer. Then when I got close enough, He took my hand and sweetly guided me into the trunk of the tree. Once inside, I saw this spiral staircase that went down for miles and miles. I could not see the end of it. I proceeded to follow Jesus all the way down to the bottom. A great surprise was waiting there. My entire family—Dad, Mom, Caleb, Rachel, Abigail, and Bart—were all at the bottom with open arms. I remember running into their arms and feeling such a joy at being with them.

Then I took some time to look around. There were roots sprouting out from everywhere. This oak tree had come to be what it was through many years of growth, and I would come to be who I needed to be by acknowledging my roots. God wanted me to see that it was time to let my roots go deeper. This was one of the main things that clearly directed my path toward going home. Then one morning, I woke up and went to spend some time with God. While in my time with God, I felt His stirring inside of me to go. This time, I simply said yes! The peace I felt inside was too incredible to describe. I knew then that I was making the decision I should have made three months prior to this time.

TRUST

Now I wish I could say that everyone was happy about my decision, that they all supported me and told me it was what I needed to do. But that wouldn't be the truth. In fact, I received opposition from every side. Yes, there were a few who strongly believed in me and the direction that God was taking me. But there were others who simply thought I was being negligent to leave such a great job behind and the security that money can bring in this world. I was told many times that I was making a bad decision. That didn't matter. Often God shows us what He wants for our lives, but doesn't always clue everyone else in. Sure, that would be nice, but it doesn't always happen.

I say this to encourage you to take every step that God asks you to take. Do not be concerned about what others think or what they say. They will never know God's plan for you. You will know it through listening to Him. I have never been disappointed in my move home to Minnesota. I have seen God restore my relationship with all my siblings and my parents. I have seen Him do a work that only He could do. I came home at a perfect time to be a part of things that God had ordained long before I even thought about returning. Yes, God does know what He's doing. Are you willing to follow Him to lands that are unknown? Are you willing to go to those lands that are familiar to you but are kind of scary to go to? It's time for us to embrace all that God wants us to be. To follow Him into the land He has so chosen for us.

In his heart a man plans his course, but the Lord determines his steps.

— Proverbs 16:9

Corrie Ten Boom once said, "Never be afraid to trust an unknown future to a known God." There really isn't anything like God's direction for our lives; trusting Him and allowing Him to take us to the places He wants us to go. I really didn't have a clue as to why God would lead me home,

TRUST

but throughout the last three years I've seen the answer clearly. God knew what would go on in my family members' lives. Some examples are a divorce between my parents, my youngest sibling almost losing his life, three of my siblings becoming clean from addictions, treatment plans with two of them, relationships with my family members that needed to grow, watching my brother become a father (the spark in his eyes cannot be denied), and most of all my roots have gone deeper into the soil. God has shown me that trusting Him with this step was one of the best things I could have ever done.

And without faith it is impossible to please God, because anyone who comes to him must believe that he exists and that he rewards those who earnestly seek him.
— Hebrews 11:6

Many people will walk in and out of your life, but only true friends will leave footprints in your heart.

—Eleanor Roosevelt

Chapter 5

FRIENDS...
JUST THE RIGHT PEOPLE
AT JUST THE RIGHT TIME

A critical area where we need to trust God is in our relationships with others. Why is this so important you might ask? Well, think of it this way: who knows you better than God? Who is better equipped to satisfy your needs and provide the right people to keep you going in the right direction? Proverbs 27:17 says, "As iron sharpens iron, so one man sharpens another." Sometimes it's difficult to choose people that will sharpen us. It's much easier to become dull spirited, than to find people who can sharpen us in godly character. God knows how important relationships are and that's why He demands so much from them.

Greater love has no one than this, that he lay down his life for his friends.

— John 15:13

All throughout my life, God has provided people to be companions, mentors, teachers, and friends to me. He has filled every empty hole in my heart when I needed someone just to encourage me along His path. He knows us so well. Why is a dog man's best friend? Because a

TRUST

dog is loyal and he would do anything for his owner. We should desire to have friendships that we can count on in this way. That's how God designed friendship.

A big part of this is letting Him choose our friends. Sure, when we're young it seems only natural to choose our own friends, but the older we get the more responsible we are for those we hang around. Letting God make the decision as to who we hang out with will keep us out of a lot of trouble. It also gives Him the opportunity to manage our friendships.

There are so many people in my life who have come to really care about me. So many times, I find myself looking in the mirror and asking why they care so much about me. I'm just me. Then God reminds me that I'm so much more in Him and friendship is a part of His design. He brings the right people into my life at the right time for any and every situation. There are so many variables in life. We can choose so many directions. And I'm not saying that all of them are good directions. When we allow God to shape and mold our friendships, we are giving Him control in one more area of our lives, which includes what we may become.

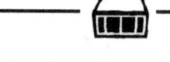

My friends have helped shape me. Their love and kindness have helped me get to where I am. I would like to say I chose each one of them very carefully, but that would not be the truth. So many

So the Lord spoke to Moses face to face, as a man speaks to his friend.

— Exodus 33:11 (NKJV)

times, I found myself just being loved by them and not even knowing from where they came. Why was this? It was because I decided a while ago that I wanted God to have even this area of my life. He called Abraham His friend. He knows how to choose friends, so I want Him to choose my friends. It's a great and wonderful place to be.

TRUST

Some relationships and friendships are only in our lives for a season. Wayne Watson once said, "God pairs people as friends at the right time and place and season of need" (quoted in Myers). I have seen many friends come and go. In the beginning I would get so frustrated because of all the effort it took to nurture a friendship. God would then remind me it wasn't mine to have and it certainly was not my decision to keep it.

Every friend has the potential to leave footprints. Every relationship can be good when God ordains the steps. Some of my first quality friends came in college during my freshman year. There were too many of them to count, but two individuals stand out in my mind. They both helped me face things that I was unwilling to face. They showed me that friendship was more than just saying you're a friend. They helped me see that you can depend on people when you first have your sights on God.

I remember one particular night when these two friends showed up in my room and I was frustrated beyond belief about things that I couldn't change. One of my friends held up a pillow and said, "Come on, hit this as hard as you can." I hit it, but not with too much force. I didn't want to look silly. She said, "Come on, I know you can do better than that." So I hit it again. I never really unleashed everything that was going on inside of me, but what I came to realize was precious in its own way.

I realized that it was okay for me to be upset and that God sends people in our path to help us get through those tough times. College took its toll on our friendship, and we ended up drifting apart. But I will never forget these two women who taught me that friendship is much more than mere acquaintance. I no longer remember what their faces look like, but I have a frame with their feet in it because they truly left footprints in my life.

TRUST

Since then, God has opened the door for me to receive from many friends. I have always tried to go to Him to seek His best, and He has always come through. There were times I needed a friend to get through a death in my family and God provided someone. There were times I needed someone to listen and help me hear what God wanted for my life. There were times I simply wanted to have fun, and God provided those people too.

I have never lacked anything in the friendship area, because I have always been willing to let God be my number one source of companionship and have only looked at everything else as an added gift. This is how we should all look at friendships. They are not ours to request, to keep, or to even let go of. They are God's, and trusting Him with the details of friendship will prove to be the only wise decision ever made.

An example of a great friendship is the friendship that David and Jonathan enjoyed in the Bible. They showed how far the depth of friendship could go and were a model of what to be as a friend. The Life Application Bible says,

> ***Their friendship is one of the deepest and closest recorded in the Bible: 1. They based their friendship on commitment to God, not just each other; 2. They let nothing come between them, not even career or family problems; 3. They drew closer together when their friendship was tested; 4. They remained friends to the end.***
> (1 Samuel 18:1–4)

This is an outline of how true friendship can and should be. Here are just a few examples of how Jonathan came through as a friend to David. In 1 Samuel 20:4 Jonathan says to David, "Whatever you want me to do, I'll do for you." Jonathan was devoted. He wanted to help his friend in every way possible because he knew David would one day be

TRUST

the king. He did not begrudge him this. Instead, he did everything in his power to help him accomplish this.

Another example of Jonathan's friendship came in 1 Samuel 23:16–17,

> ***And Saul's son Jonathan went to David at Horesh and helped him find strength in God. "Don't be afraid," he said. "My father Saul will not lay a hand on you. You will be king over Israel, and I will be second to you …"***

Jonathan believed in David and encouraged him to continue his walk in God. We need to continuously surround ourselves with people who will encourage us to be all that we can be in God.

He who walks with the wise grows wise, but a companion of fools suffers harm.
— Proverbs 13:20

After Jonathan died, David expressed his grief over the loss of his friend. He said, "I grieve for you, Jonathan my brother; you were very dear to me. Your love for me was wonderful, more wonderful than that of women." (2 Samuel 1:26) David mourned the loss, as anyone would mourn the loss of a brother. This is how close we should be as friends. The only way we can experience this depth in friendship is by allowing God to partner us with people who encourage us in life's travels. We also hold an obligation to our friends to be sincere, honest, loving, encouraging, and refining.

Proverbs 17:17 says, "A friend loves at all times…" We need to love our friends even when we don't understand them and help them see who God is at all times. "As iron sharpens iron, so one man sharpens another." (Proverbs 27:17) Are you feeling sharpened by your friends and are you taking a responsibility to sharpen them? It's time we start experiencing friendships in a deeper way. God's way!

It is impossible to win the race unless you venture to run, impossible to win the victory, unless you dare to battle.

—Richard M. DeVos

Chapter 6

Victory in the Battles

Trust in the Lord and do good; dwell in the land and enjoy safe pasture. (Psalm 37:3) We have explored the areas in which we need to trust God. I pray that these words will take meaning in your life and that you will find yourself entrusting God with even the smallest of details. He has certainly proven to be worthy of your trust.

The last part of this verse talks about dwelling in the land and enjoying safe pasture. You might ask what this means. What I think about when I read it is the many

The Lord is my shepherd, I shall not be in want.
— Psalm 23:1

times that Jesus talks about being a Shepherd to the flock. We are a part of that flock. God is watching over us and only wants us to relax. Enjoy what He has given you, don't take it for granted. See it for what it is. Let God give you peace in all of your circumstances. When you allow yourself to entrust Him with the details of your life, you will see how easy it is to simply enjoy safe pasture.

Let me share a story with you about a woman who put her trust in God, despite her own lack of strength to do so. Jesus told Paul, "My grace is sufficient for you; for my power is made perfect in weakness." (2 Corinthians 12:9) Annie Johnson Flint lived out a life that exhibits strength beyond her ability. She experienced God's perfection through her weakness.

Her story is quite vast, and I encourage you to read about it. I will only give some brief highlights from it. As a young girl, she lost her birth parents. Later, in her high school years, she lost her adopted parents. During this time, she was stricken with a terrible case of arthritis. It slowly crept into her system and took away her ability to be mobile. Doctors had told her that she would be an invalid and that she would be unable to care for herself. Soon she became bed ridden and all she could do was write poetry. Many days she would be in pain too terrible to describe, yet she would have someone put a pen in her hand and write praises to God.

The pen pushed through her bent fingers and held by her swollen joints wrote numerous praises to God. At first she just used it as an outlet to express herself. She never dreamed that it would one day bring her financial support or would live on after her death. She wrote because her trust in God needed to be expressed and the best way she could do this was through her poems. She also made cards, gift books, hymns, and even decorated some of her own verses. She did all this throughout her time in pain.

There were days she would wake up and not be able to move her head without pain, yet she still found a means to write. During the times she had the finances to pay for someone to come into her home, she would dictate her poetry for her caretaker to write down. Her words resonate with truth that only comes from a heart that found peace in God. She could have given up and just wasted away in her

These things I have spoken to you, so that in Me you may have peace. In the world you have tribulation, but take courage; I have overcome the world.
— John 16:33 (NASB)

bed. That might have been what I would have done, but she could not dream of this. She wanted to praise God for who He was despite the circumstances that surrounded her life.

All too often, we become good at expressing our thankfulness to God when things are going good, but we forget to praise Him through the bad times. You can look at every poem that Annie wrote and see the glimmer of hope that must have sparkled in her eyes. It can't be hidden. It is so obvious that it often makes me wonder what I would do if in the same position.

One of her many poems that truly has been a blessing to me is called "Better than My Best." The words throughout it describe a life abandoned to the purpose of God; a heart that is sold out for Him. Read this portion of the poem and let these words sink into your soul. May your heart feel what Annie was trying to express when she wrote of her love for God even through the agony she faced on a daily basis.

> ***But while the battle raged, and wild winds blew,***
> ***I heard His voice and perfect peace I knew.***
> ***I thank you, Lord, You were too wise to heed***
> ***My feeble prayers, and answer as I sought,***
> ***Since these rich gifts Your bounty has bestowed***
> ***Have brought me more than all I asked or thought;***
> ***Giver of good, so answer each request***
> ***With your own giving, better than my best.***

—Annie Johnson Flint

These words only skim the top of what Annie's example can teach so many. Trusting God doesn't mean that we have to understand what He's doing. It simply means we have to give up trying to figure it out. It's not meant for us to figure out. God is the Author of your story, and He is writing a book to which only He knows the ending. Life might

TRUST

throw you some earth shattering news, but remember God is in the storm. He is there to lead you out. He will be your strength when you are too weak to carry on. Let God's power be made perfect in your weakness.

Choose to dwell in the land. May you experience unspeakable joy through any suffering you may have to go through in this lifetime. Also, I sincerely hope that you will see God going before you into all your battles.

Find rest, O my soul, in God alone; my hope comes from him.
— Psalm 62:5

May you see that He alone will bring victory to the war that rages around you, and may you choose to praise Him through the trials in your life. May you be able to rest in the love of your Father who is all knowing and perfect in every way. Last but not least, spend time resting in the land and let God restore you, so you might be able to fully delight yourself in Him. Rest in the area in which God has placed you. Allow Him to be the rock on which you stand.

Let Everything That Has Breath Praise the Lord

PSALM 150:6

Father in Heaven! When the thought of thee wakes in our hearts, let it not awaken like a frightened bird that flies about in dismay, but like a child waking from sleep with a heavenly smile.

—Soren Kierkegaard

Chapter 7
DADDY, DADDY

The next part of Psalm 37 says, "Delight yourself in the Lord and He will give you the desires of your heart." (Psalm 37:4) Boy, doesn't this sound simple? Can it possibly be that easy to receive the desires of our hearts? Well, I think we can receive the desires of our hearts when we first align ourselves with God's Word and do what He requires from us. The first thing we need to do is trust Him with every detail of our life ... not just the major details, but the minor ones also. We must let Him be Lord over every decision. This naturally leads us into a place where we desire to simply delight ourselves in Him.

I remember when I was just starting a new job. My boss was teaching me some things on the computer when his wife and two daughters came into the office. They were out in the hallway, and we were in one of the side rooms. I remember that before they came, his focus was completely on teaching me the task at hand, but

Trust God from the bottom of your heart; don't try to figure out everything on your own. Listen for God's voice in everything you do, everywhere you go; he's the one who will keep you on track.
— Proverbs 3:5-6 (*MSG*)

that all changed when his little girls showed up. His little girl Bailey kept saying, "Daddy, Daddy." She was trying desperately to get his attention from quite a distance away, and she definitely had achieved her goal.

DELIGHT

He could no longer focus on the task at hand. All he could do was think about that little voice that kept calling out his name. He said, "I'm so sorry, I just can't concentrate. The sound of her voice makes me so happy." He grinned from ear to ear and let her know that she could come in and sit on his lap. From that time on, he was more focused and was able to finish teaching me what I needed to know on the program.

After he left, I remember crying and thanking God for showing me something so special in that moment. Not only does the sound of that little girl's voice catch her daddy's attention, but the sound of my voice brings a smile to my Heavenly Father's face, too. God showed me in that moment how much He loves it when I call His name.

The Lord your God is in your midst, a Warrior who saves. He will rejoice over you with joy; He will be quiet in His love [making no mention of your past sins], He will rejoice over you with shouts of joy.
— Zephaniah 3:17 (*AMP*)

He is delighted by the times that I simply say, "Daddy, I need You. I love You. Can You be there for me? Can I sit on Your knee?" Those times are so valuable to God because in those moments everything else ceases to be in my mind. My only desire is to delight myself in Him by sitting on His knee and basking in His presence. I learned a valuable lesson that day. My desires do not simply come to pass because I want them to come. No, they are given to me through the Father's gentle hand when I surrender myself to Him and simply delight in His way alone.

This is a wonderful place to find ourselves. To know that God cares about the simple desires of our heart, as well as the big desires. I find that my value in God has always been priceless, but I've never been able to comprehend it. I have never been able to see myself as someone worthy of complete value. This might sound a little sad, but it's true. I can come up with all my faults and lay them out pretty well.

DELIGHT

Through this process, I seem to lose value in myself. Yet in spite of myself, God has taken the time to show me my immense value in Him. To put down in words everything that He has used to show me this would fill up a whole new book.

One way that God has shown me the depth of my worth is through a vacation I took in 2005. I was able to go see Niagara Falls. What a grand scene! Nothing compares to it! I looked at the falls with great admiration for the Lord, as His magnificent work of art left me speechless. Every intricate detail was so well woven into this picture before me. Every intricately placed rock amazed me. The height of the falls and the incredible design of the great expanse before me, both left me in awe. The rainbow that always seems to appear over it, the sound of the water falling, and the fresh air from the breeze left me with an inescapable sense of wonder. Everything about it was too amazing for words. I was taking in every moment of it and trying to capture it in my heart. My memory loves to take pictures that I can pull up later and see. This time taking pictures was a little more difficult as there was so much to capture in a small amount of time.

Charles Dickens once visited the Niagara Falls and after his experience he wrote,

> *It was not until I came on Table Rock and looked—Great Heaven, on what a fall of bright green water!—That it came upon me in its full might and majesty. Then, when I felt how near to my Creator I was standing, the first effect, and enduring one—instant and lasting—of the tremendous spectacle, was Peace. Peace of Mind, tranquility, calm recollections of the Dead, great thoughts of Eternal Rest and Happiness: nothing of gloom or terror. Niagara was at once stamped upon my heart, an Image of Beauty; to remain there, changeless and indelible, until its pulses cease to beat, forever.*

DELIGHT

I love the way this author expresses himself after he takes in the falls and their charm. He describes in words what I'm still trying to conceive of in my mind. During this time at the falls, God pressed on my heart how much He truly values me. Though I looked at these falls with such adoration and awe for what they were, God still looked at me as so much more than that. Niagara Falls has been flowing for many years. God set it up, He designed every detail of it, and now it simply flows on its own. It doesn't take a lot of work to maintain such a grand scene. Yes, human beings try to corrupt it, but for the most part it just continues to fall in all its splendor.

I know that in my life God is working on a daily basis to make a masterpiece out of me. No artist is ever quite satisfied with their painting or drawing. There is always something to fix or change a little bit. I know this because I watch my dad work on drawings for a year or so. I look at them each

He has made everything beautiful in its time. He has also set eternity in the hearts of men; yet they cannot fathom what God has done from beginning to end.
— Ecclesiastes 3:11

time and think, "Wow, that is so cool." He looks at it and thinks "Well, this needs to be shaded in a little bit, and this isn't quite even." I think he should invest stock in erasers, as I have never seen anyone use an eraser as much as he does.

There are so many details he sees that I don't because I don't work on the drawing. He is the one with the pencil. Often, I try to remember that God is the one with the pencil writing out the story of my life. He is weaving details in and out all the time that I can't begin to understand. He is changing things in me on a moment by moment basis. I remember taking a walk one day and expressing to God my desire to be with someone who was in my life. God simply showed me

DELIGHT

that I could take the pencil and write the story, but the ending would not be as beautiful as the one He has created for me. He showed me that He wants to be the one to write my story, so I simply gave up my pencil. I could have played tug of war with Him, but we all know how that would have ended. I'm no competition for the Creator Himself.

Isaiah 64:8 says, "Yet, O Lord, you are our Father. We are the clay, you are the potter; we are all the work of your hand." I don't know about you, but I love this picture. I am not a product of my own design or plan. I am a product of the Master's hand. What a thought! I mean every day God is working in me to create a masterpiece, like the masterpiece I see when I look at Niagara Falls. His hand shapes me and molds me. It makes me into His likeness and creates in me a desire to delight myself in Him.

I remember one time in a college class we were asked to spend some time with our eyes shut and just focus on God. We were told to just let God show us whatever He wanted to show us. At first it was tough for me to quiet every thought running rampant through my mind. Then after a little while the wheels of my brain slowed down, and my concentration was fully on the Author of my life. I saw a picture that I had never seen before. There before me was a pot made from clay spinning on the potter's wheel. I saw myself working so hard to make it into a perfect little pot.

Sweat was pouring down my brow, as I was working with all my might to make it into a work of art. Then out of no where I saw these two hands reach down and gently grab mine. They worked with me to form the pot. It was as if God was saying to me that I was not the one writing this story. He was writing it. I needed to slow down and let Him define me through every groove that He so gently worked into my being. I needed to hand over the keys of my responsibilities to Him and see how He wanted to work through them.

DELIGHT

Madeleine L'Engle once said, "Someone has altered the script. My lines have been changed ... I thought I was writing the play." Yes, it's so easy to want to take the pen and write the story of our lives. I mean I know that I have great potential in God to be whatever He has designed me to be, but I'm still incapable of writing the story of my life. I don't know how the details fit in. I'm not sure why things happen like they do.

Often, I think, "Okay, God, how are you going to use this for your good?" Then God surprises me. He always shows up in my circumstances and helps me reach far past what I would consider reaching for. I have limitations because I am formed as human, but God has no limitations when it comes to designing the details of my life. He never runs out of paper to write on and He never runs out of plans to perform in my life. He is truly mysterious in all that He does, but part of the beauty in life thrives on this mystery that is found in Him.

And we know that in all things God works for the good of those who love him, who have been called according to his purpose.
— Romans 8:28

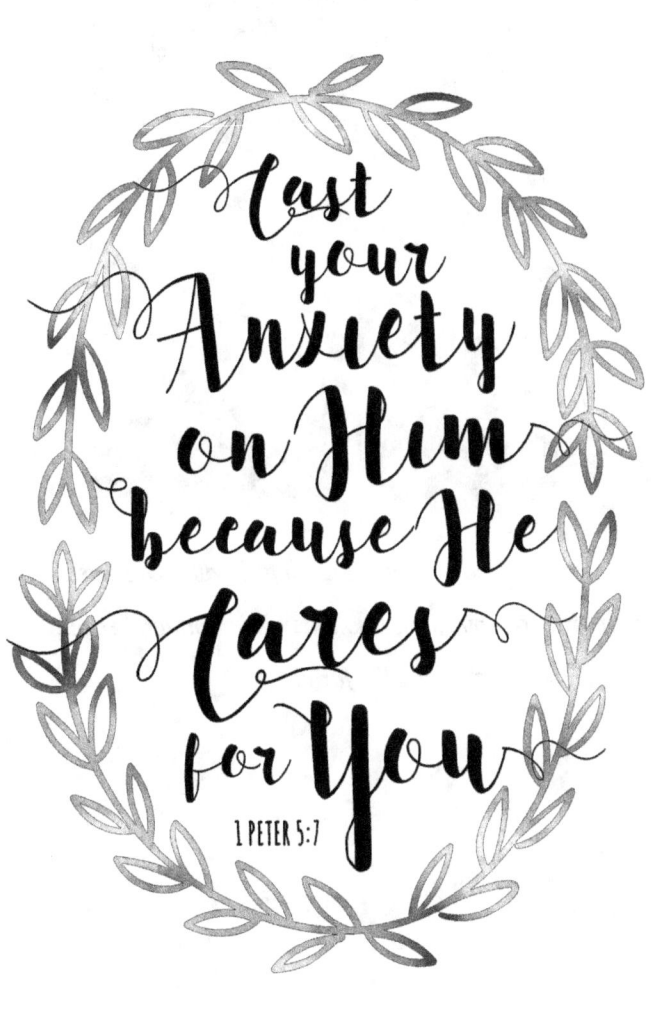

God has given me this day to use it as I will. I can waste it—or use it for good, but what I do today is important, because I am exchanging a day of my life for it!

—Heartsill Wilson

Chapter 8
TIME IS NOT OURS

Hebrews 12:2 says, "Let us fix our eyes on Jesus, the author and perfecter of our faith, who for the joy set before Him endured the cross, scorning it's shame and sat down at the right hand of the throne of God." This verse clearly shares who the Author and Perfecter of our faith is. This is a loaded verse in so many ways. First, what can we do to fix our eyes on God, so that our desires simply line up with His heart for us? Second, how can we let Him be the Author and Perfecter of our faith? Lastly, how can we consider recognizing all that Christ did when He embraced the cross for our sake?

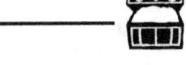

Well, fixing our eyes on God can be a very difficult thing. Sometimes I wish I had the blinders that horses wear to keep their eyes looking straight ahead. They don't look to the left or the right. They simply keep their course and go after what it is they want. This is how I want to be. I want to fix my eyes on God. I believe we can do this on a daily basis.

I run in the path of your commands, for you have set my heart free.

— Psalm 119:32

One way that I do this is by waking up every morning and simply declaring, "This is your day, God; I am here because You have me here.

DELIGHT

Please help me to be aware of Your purpose for me today and to walk it out fully. May I stay on the path on which You have called me forward." Also, all throughout the day I carry on a constant conversation with God. I share with Him my desires, my needs, my hurts, my joys, my letdowns, my hang-ups, my fumbles, and essentially my everything.

In the Bible, David was in constant communication with God. Yes, he made some unwise moves, but he always came faithfully back to God. I want to be a woman after God's own heart: one who seeks out God's desires alone and not my own.

David declares, "Then I will go to the altar of God, to God, my joy and my delight. I will praise you with the harp, O God, my God." (Psalm 43:4) David declared that God was his delight. He made music to Him and let his heart worship the One who made Him. When was the last time you simply stopped to make music to the Lord? When was the last time you declared Him to be your joy and delight? Do you know He longs to hear these words from you?

Praise the Lord with the harp; Make melody to Him with an instrument of ten strings. Sing to Him a new song; Play skillfully with a shout of joy
— Psalm 33:2-3 (NKJV)

I'm not saying you have to play the harp or any instrument at all. The greatest instrument you have is your heart! Let God simply play your heart strings. Let Him show you the ways that you can delight yourself in Him. A few months ago, I went for a walk and on my way home I was passing by a retirement home. A little old man waved from his bedroom window, and I felt the urge to go in and say hi. Yes, time was limited. There was so much I wanted to get done, but I knew I needed to take that moment to go in and express love to that man. Little did I know that someone else would be waiting at the door for me who also needed to experience love, if even for a moment.

DELIGHT

I first sat and talked to a lovely lady, who expressed to me that no one ever has the time to stop by any more. She talked about her children and said that they were busy. She told me about her golden years and how they didn't feel so golden. In her words, "The golden years are tarnished." Throughout the conversation, I saw her little heart come alive just because someone stopped to say hi. We talked about playing cards, and I will stop by to see her again. Then, I was on to my original reason for knocking on the door.

I walked down the hallway to see a man, lying in his bed, not able to hear much of what I was saying, but that didn't matter because all he wanted to do was give me an ear full. He talked and talked. I sat and listened. He told me that he's lonely and that people don't stop by to see him. He said everyone was busy. In that moment, I thought who are we to decide what we get to do with our time? We don't make time, so why do we get to decide how to use it? This man expressed how happy he was that I stopped by and that it was so nice to see that someone wasn't in a hurry to just do what they had to do.

The truth is, in the back of my mind, I was somewhat thinking of everything I had to do before the night ended, but somewhere in that room I lost the sense of time and just enjoyed being there for a man who simply needed someone to listen. Have you ever thought of playing music like this for God? I often do. God reminds me every so often to slow down, enjoy life, and let Him direct those steps. Loving people is a great way to delight yourself in Him. Not only do you have the opportunity to express the Father's heart to someone in need, but you also have the opportunity to feel what the Father feels for you every time you need Him to stop and listen.

God never sees time as an obstacle. We, however, have almost come to see it as our enemy. Twenty-four hours just doesn't seem long enough, but how wrong is it to think that way. God made the day the way that

DELIGHT

He made it because He knew we would need to rest at times too. Yes, time is certainly an area where we can delight ourselves in the Lord.

I challenge you to stop today and find someone to love on. Show them who God is through a simple hello or a simple smile. Don't be afraid to take five minutes to slow down. God will help you get done what you need to get done. Fix your eyes on Him, line up your thoughts with His thoughts, and see what He can do with your time. I mean it really is His time that we are living on and we should let Him direct the day's activities.

Sow for yourselves righteousness; reap in mercy; break up your fallow ground, for it is time to seek the Lord, till He comes and rains righteousness on you.
— Hosea 10:12 (NKJV)

YOU ARE THE LIGHT
of the world

MATTHEW 5:14

Why did the achievers overcome problems while thousands are overwhelmed by theirs? They refused to hold on to the common excuses for failure. They turned their stumbling blocks into stepping stones. They realized that they couldn't determine every circumstance in life but they could determine their choice of attitude towards every circumstance.

—John C. Maxwell

Chapter 9

REFOCUSING THE VIEW

Okay, now what? How can we let God be the Author and Perfecter of our faith? This is a great question. Let's explore the answer. Get your tools. We're going to dig a little deeper and find out what it means to really give God the place of authorship in our lives. First, we must find out what we are hungering after. Matthew 5:6 says, "Blessed are those who hunger and thirst for righteousness, for they will be filled." We were put on this earth to hunger for righteousness.

All too often we hunger for more time and thirst for more money. We want what we do not have and forget to be thankful for what we do have. I've done it a thousand times. This verse comes back to me and shows me that hungering and thirsting for the things of this world will not satisfy me. My needs are simply met when I hunger and thirst for righteousness. Righteousness simply means, "Meeting the standards of what is right and just: morally right." (Webster's Dictionary) Do you hunger for what is right?

Have you ever become so thirsty that you just simply wanted a glass of water and you would do almost anything for it, but you

He who pursues righteousness and love finds life, prosperity and honor.

— Proverbs 21:21

DELIGHT

were in a place that no water could be found? I've been there. It's a terrible feeling to thirst and not be able to quench that thirst. Well, living for God means that we are constantly hungry and thirsty for the things of God. It's a place where we desire to do His will and honestly place Him before anything else. In Him, every desire can be met. Without Him, every desire is empty.

Thankfully, thirsting after the things of God is not like thirsting for water because God continuously meets our needs. I remember one particular instance when I was thirsty; I needed more of God. I had been so drained that I felt like everyone in my life needed something and I had nothing left to give. I went for a long walk and shared with God how I felt so empty inside. He showed me a well, and that well was empty. I went to draw water from it and something remarkable happened. Water appeared in the bucket that I lifted from the bottom of the well. But I saw no water in the bottom of that well. God simply showed me. That's the point! The water we search for in this world is empty, but God is endlessly filling us up with Himself when we fix our eyes on Him.

Jesus answered, "Everyone who drinks this water will be thirsty again, but whoever drinks the water I give him will never thirst. Indeed, the water I give him will become in him a spring of water welling up to eternal life.

— John 4:13-14

Jeremiah 2:13 says, "My people have committed two sins: They have forsaken me, the spring of living water, and have dug their own cisterns, broken cisterns that cannot hold water." We ourselves cannot contain the water that is talked about in the Word of God. It is too much for us to handle. We try to build wells for it and try to come up with places to store it, but we build with human hands. God simply comes into our lives and says, "Let me build the well. I will fill it up with

DELIGHT

water that is pure." Let His pure water fill your soul and let Him empty out the garbage that simply doesn't belong there.

Another way we can give ourselves over to this Author of our lives is by simply learning to focus on what is important and letting everything else just fade away. In the movie *For Love of the Game*, Kevin Costner's character had a strategy on how to focus while on the pitcher's mound. He stands with his ball in his glove and simply says, "Clear the mechanism." As he says this, you can see everything fade away from view, except the catcher and the catcher's glove. We need to clear the mechanism, let everything else fade out of view, and simply focus on what God puts before us.

In college I would go for walks with a friend. We would talk and talk, but every once in a while one of those air pockets would sneak up on me and I would go tumbling to the ground. She would get a good laugh out of it and I would simply joke, "That's my gracefulness for you." All too often I fell because I was looking up at the stars or at the view around me. I would get caught up in the scenery and forget what I was doing. Each time I did this, my humility was increased. The good side of falling is that humility is increased each time you fall.

One day I realized that I needed to stay more focused on what was ahead of me and less focused on what was around me. Through this I learned another very valuable lesson. I fall less when my focus is on God. My run in Him increases when my eyes are set upon His desires and not my own. I tend to go at a steady and even pace when I focus in on Him.

...for though a righteous man falls seven times, he rises again, but the wicked are brought down by calamity.
— Proverbs 24:16

DELIGHT

This is where I find myself saying, "Lord, I want to be someone who delights in you, not because I want these desires that are in my heart, but essentially because you are worthy, worthy of my praise. May I find myself resting in You and seeking Your purpose." In saying this over and over again I see the desires of my heart come about, not because I went seeking after them, but because I put God first and put my desires second to Him. Often my desires change as I become more refined in Him. This is a great thing because He knows what is better for me than I do.

So how can we let God be the Author and Perfecter of our faith? That's a great question. I think it is answered over and over again in the Bible. The study of each character shows the total dependence on God and the lack of dependence on self. One look at the Faith Hall of Fame in Hebrews chapter 11 will tell you all those who let God be the Author and Perfecter of their faith.

Hebrews 11 starts out by saying, "Now faith is being sure of what we hope for and certain of what we do not see." I don't know about you, but there are many times I desire things that are far from my sight spiritually, and yet they come to fruition. Some characters in the Bible who had to wait a long while to see their desires fulfilled were: Noah, Abraham, Joseph, and Moses. The list could go on and on. Each one was told something would happen but lived a long time to see the result. In some cases the result would not be seen while living their earthly lives, but they didn't give up hope. They continued to fix their eyes on God and followed through on what He asked of them, simply because He asked it.

Noah built the ark even though he had never heard of a thing called rain. Abraham left his home for a land he had never seen before. He also trusted in God for a son, even into his old age. Joseph had a dream in the very beginning of his life that pointed to some very sure things

DELIGHT

in the future, but that future was a little farther off than he would have expected. Moses was called to lead the Israelites into the land God promised for them, but he never even got to enter the land.

These four men exhibited a focus that could not be shaken. They were focused on delighting themselves in God, so consequently He could follow through on the desires He had for their lives. When our focus is on God and all that He has in store for us, our desires start to line up with His. It's like two roads converging. You can't keep them from converging and once they do, they go on forever. God's desires and our desires need to be in alignment so that we can better serve Him with our talents. He is the Author and the Perfecter of our faith, not because we determine that, but because He decided to be that for us.

Joseph said, *"You intended to harm me, but God intended it for good to accomplish what is now being done, the saving of many lives."*

— Genesis 50:20

While we may not be called to martyr our lives, we must martyr our way of life. We must put our selfish ways to death and march to a different beat. Then the world will see Jesus.

—Michael Tait

Chapter 10
LIVING THE LIFE

We have now found out what we can do to fix our eyes on God. We've also looked into how we can make Him the Author and Perfecter of our faith. But this isn't the end of the story. No, this is just the beginning. The rest of Hebrews 12:2 says, " … who for the joy set before Him endured the cross, scorning its shame and sat down at the right hand of the throne of God." How can we embrace what Christ did on the cross?

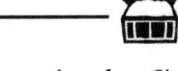

Christ embraced the cross for each one of us so that we would one day be able to live to our greatest potential in the Father. He counted it as joy, not because it wasn't painful, but because the result was endless. Eternity was set aside for

We are therefore Christ's ambassadors, as though God were making his appeal through us.…

— 2 Corinthians 5:20

each one of us because we're worth it, not because of whom we are or what we do, but because of who He is and what He does in each one of us. How can we embrace this truth on a daily basis? My answer to this is simple. Share what you have. Don't keep it inside. God has called you to be an ambassador for Christ's sake. Webster's dictionary defines ambassador as "an authorized representative or messenger." You and I are authorized to go and share the precious gift that has been given to each one of us.

DELIGHT

You may ask, "How can I do this?" Some will say they don't have the courage. Others will say they are too tired. Some will say they just don't have the words, while others do have the words and just don't want to be looked at in a negative way. Remember this: being an ambassador for Christ is simple. You have the choice to do it every day.

The first simple thing that you can do is wear a smile. Show the world that you are joyful and that you have meaning. Make them wonder why it is you can smile so much and what it is about you that's so different. Second of all, open your mouth. Let the words pour forth. No, you don't have to be all eloquent in your speech or say just the right thing. Sometimes a simple "Hello," "Thank you" or "Can I help you with that?" opens a door to a conversation that will shed light on who God is inside of you. Remember that we are called to be examples for Him, people living for His purpose and not our own.

One thing I find I love to do that really opens the door for God to work is filling the need wherever it may be. Open a door for a stranger. Help someone reach something in the grocery store when they are unable to. Offer to be a listening ear when people need to express what they are feeling. There have been so many cool situations that God has used me in to really exhibit His love towards people.

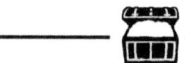

A merry heart does good, like medicine, but a broken spirit dries the bones.
— Proverbs 17:22 (NKJV)

I was once in a rest area where there was a food court. I was sitting with some friends and just doing a little people watching. Across the room I saw a lady with her two kids scrambling to get to a table. In the midst of her scrambling, she spilled the pop she had just bought for all of them. She looked around nervously seeking relief, but none came. I simply got up from my table and walked to hers with some napkins in hand to help her clean up the mess.

DELIGHT

She was so grateful. The smile on her face was worth a thousand words. She expressed how thankful she was and more than anything her appearance changed. I wish I could describe the look on her face when I started to help her clean up the mess because I think it would motivate us all to help others. It's a simple thing. It didn't take any time at all. It didn't cost me a thing. But, boy, did I feel rewarded when I walked away.

Another time, I remember being with some friends from high school coming back from a retreat in Colorado. We were standing in line at a fast food restaurant. One lady came up to dump her tray in the garbage can, but missed it. Everything spilled on the floor. I simply got down and helped her place everything back on the tray to go in the garbage.

She too was grateful. Her face expressed what she could not say. Her depth of gratitude could not be measured. Did I do anything great or worthy of attention? No, not really. I simply filled the need. I know that is why we are on this earth. We are here to fill the need, to be the friend, to be the one who goes the extra mile, to be the one who helps when everyone else just laughs. We are called to be ambassadors for Christ sharing His love with others even in its simplest form.

Dear children, let us not love with words or tongue but with actions and in truth.

— 1 John 3:18

Now don't get me wrong, there are times to share the message of His love in even greater ways. I could share quite a few of these with you too, but that is not the message I'm trying to get across. I want you to simply know that your every action speaks volumes of who God is inside of you. A simple thank you will put a smile on a cashier's face

DELIGHT

when all she has had is complaining customers all day long. So next time you are standing in line at the grocery store, don't forget to ask how the cashier is doing. Let him or her know that you value what they do and simply express that through your act of kindness.

be Devoted to one another in Love

If I find in myself desires which nothing in this world can satisfy, the only logical explanation is that I was made for another world.

—C. S. Lewis

Chapter 11

AN EAGLE'S FLIGHT

Delight yourself in the Lord and He will give you the desires of your heart. (Psalm 37:4) Once we completely delight ourselves in God and His ways, then and only then can the desires of our heart be met. Why is this? Well, let's find out and in the midst of the search let's tap into those desires that lay deep inside our hearts.

What should be our ultimate desire? It should be a desire to follow after God with all that we are of course. David declares, "I desire to do your will, O my God; your law is within my heart" (Psalm 40:8). I have tried so hard to make this my number one desire. I can tell you that some days I do great at it and other days I struggle. Ultimately, God is faithful in being patient with me, as I walk along this road with Him. He sees me get off track at times and desire things that I really don't need, but He is faithful to bring me back.

One of the many times I got off track was when I got into my first relationship. I desired companionship so much that I let it override my common sense. I remember the day I completely looked to God for answers. I

I seek you with all my heart; do not let me stray from your commands.

— Psalm 119:10

wanted to make sure that it was okay to go down the road of this particular relationship. That might sound strange to some, but I was determined to make every moment count and I didn't want to be with someone who would steal away any moments that were meant for God.

I remember walking and walking and the same thing kept coming to mind. A verse I had heard over and over again. " 'For I know the plans I have for you,' declares the Lord, 'plans to prosper you and not to harm you, plans to give you a hope and a future.'" (Jeremiah 29:11) I didn't know how to respond to this as I have heard this verse many times before. It's been one of my mottos throughout life. I've known the ins and outs of it, so why was it coming up now?

The answer didn't come right away. In fact, I remember falling to my knees in a pile of dirt and just saying, "God, if this is You, let me know, but if it's not You, I'm not taking one more step into it." At that moment, I saw myself falling into a black hole. I did not see what I was falling into, and I really had no idea what it meant. I just kept falling backwards with a feeling that there would be nothing to catch me. Then in that moment, God shared another verse with me. "Be still and know that I am God." (Psalm 46:10) This verse quieted the storm that was raging inside of me. I was trying so hard not to make a mistake, that I was forgetting who God is and how He leads my steps.

I left that place feeling at peace and knowing that it was okay to enter this new relationship. It was my first, so I had no idea how it would go. All I knew was that God had given me peace to walk in it. I walked in it for two months. I know that's nothing compared to what some people have had to go through to find out that something isn't exactly what they signed up for. I don't pretend to know all the answers, and because of my humanness I can only comprehend so much.

DELIGHT

In two months, God showed me many things about myself and how I needed to heal in more areas of which I was unaware. At one point, I remember being in the bathroom at work and cleaning the shower. God refreshed my memory and showed me a dream that I had dreamed when I lived in Delaware.

The dream was pretty simple and at the time that I had the dream, no answer came as to why I had dreamed it. So I simply let it go, knowing that God would reveal the interpretation of it in due time. Well, almost six months later, the answer did come. God showed me that it had to do with this relationship. I thought it meant that I should stay in this relationship, but that's not what God was saying. See I had my ears half open to what He wanted to say and half open to what I wanted to hear.

So you may be asking what this dream was all about. Well, let me share it with you. I had a dream that I went fishing with my dad.

We seemed to have a great time together, like always. There is nothing unusual about that. Then, instead of driving home together we took separate vehicles. I went one direction, and he went another. The direction that I went brought about a beautiful surprise. That surprise was a huge eagle that swooped down in front of my car. I saw every detail of that eagle: the wing span, the eyes, the feathers, and the whole magnificent structure of that eagle. I continued to drive in the direction of that eagle, and then I woke up. Now this is very significant because both my dad and I really have a high appreciation of eagles. I kept thinking while I was watching this eagle swoop by, *Where is my dad? He would love to see this.* But he was no where to be found.

I tried to figure this dream out and in the process I asked many people what their opinion was about it. Every opinion led me in a different direction because sometimes God shares something with me that

DELIGHT

is only meant to be between the two of us. I finally came to a point where I realized that it was just another piece of the puzzle leading me home to Minnesota and that was the only answer I was going to get for now.

"For my thoughts are not your thoughts, nor are your ways My ways," declares the Lord.
— Isaiah 55:8 (NASB)

Then, there I was six months later, cleaning the shower and going about my own business. I had somewhat forgotten about that dream so it surprised me when it came back to mind. Well, I felt God share with me that it was about my new relationship and instead of listening for more details from God I interpreted it as my heart wanted to interpret it. My interpretation was that I would be spending the rest of my life with this person. That seemed like the only logical explanation to me, but logic comes from a human way of thinking, not God's way of thinking. In fact, God's logic would turn out to be so much better than my own. That should be of no surprise to any of us!

I walked away from work that day thinking I knew the answers. I knew what the desire of my heart was, and I assumed God was just going along with it. Little did I know that He had something better in store for me. Eventually, I ended up seeing that this wasn't what God had for me. I had to make the tough decision of letting go of the relationship. The freedom I felt after making the decision was too immense to describe. In just a short time all kinds of questions about my decision to be in this relationship were formed in my mind. I asked God over and over again what all my times with Him meant: the time on my walk and showing me the great black hole, knowing the plans for me, and my eagle dream. What was the real significance behind all of them? I spent many days seeking God on this and spending time in solitude. I just wanted to find out what it all meant.

DELIGHT

First, God showed me that He did know the plans for me. He knew how far and how long I would be in a relationship and He knew how He would use it to further my growth in Him. It's amazing what God can do when we open up the door of our hearts for Him to lead us. Second, God showed me what the rest of the black hole experience was all about. Throughout my time with this man I felt like I was falling backwards and no one was there to catch me. I wanted someone to show me it was okay to end it, but that someone didn't come. Well, not in the form I was expecting it. Because you see, God was there all along. Every moment of it He walked with me. And now that I had time to listen, just listen, I was able to see what was at the bottom of that big black hole.

Out of nowhere appeared a great big hand, and I simply fell into it. It was there all along. God was there! Psalm 37:23–24 says, "If the Lord delights in a man's way, He makes his steps firm; though he stumble, he will not fall, for the Lord upholds him with His hand." God had certainly upheld me with His hand. I never saw it coming, but it was there all along. It's so good to know that God does not leave just because we stop listening. I know that I had continued to try and find out what God was saying throughout my relationship, but like I said, I was listening with ears that wanted to hear things a certain way. This is where it is so important for us to let go of our own desires and simply let God fill our hearts with His desires for our lives. Our desires will always fall short of everything that He wants for us.

Great is the Lord and most worthy of praise; his greatness no one can fathom.

— Psalm 145:3

The dream of the eagle came to make sense too, but perhaps you have already figured this out. It's not that hard to see now why I went through what I went through. I saw something attractive, an opportunity to fill that part of my life. I liked the idea of being cared

DELIGHT

about and having someone to talk to at night. It led me down a completely different road though. Originally, God had called me home to simply spend time with my family, and I had found something else to follow. Thankfully, God didn't let me escape the world in which He had chosen for me to live.

This is only one of many examples that God has used to truly show me how important it is to listen to every word and find out what He is saying in everything. Don't let your mind fill in the missing pieces, instead wait for the answers. God gave us the sensation to desire things so that we could fully serve Him. Every desire needs to line up with Him.

It's easy to half-heartedly hear God when we are determined to hear things the way we want to hear them. I simply ask that you put your human ears aside. Let your every desire fade away, as you simply put your focus back on God. Let Him shape your desires so that they line up with His best for you. Trust me, no one knows you better and no one will better meet your needs than Him.

Yes, Lord, walking in the way of your laws, we wait or you; your name and renown are the desire of our hearts.
— Isaiah 26:8

Matthew Henry's commentary shares this about Psalm 37:4.

He has not promised to gratify all the appetites of the body and the humors of the fancy, but to grant all the desires of the heart, all the cravings of the renewed sanctified soul. What is the desire of the heart of a good man? It is this, to know, and love, and live, to God, to please Him and to be pleased in Him.

DELIGHT

Desiring Him first and letting everything else come into place should be the major desire that our hearts long for, then everything else will simply fall into place. The next time you're upset about God not meeting a desire in your life, ask yourself this:

Does it matter?
Is it **E**ssential?
Will it help you **S**eek Him?
Is it a good or bad **I**nfluence?
Does it cause **R**enewal in you?
Who is it an **E**xpression of; you or Jesus in you?

Commit to the Lord whatever you do, and your plans will succeed.

—Proverbs 16:3

Chapter 12
Finding True North

We have gone through quite a bit to get to this point. We have explored the need to trust God with everything, then we went into how to simply dwell in the land. The road didn't end there though. We continued to follow it through the steps of delighting ourselves in God and finding out what His desires are for our lives. Now we are coming to an overpass. At least this is how I look at it. I look at commitment as an overpass because it can be an uphill battle at times, but it's in rising above our circumstances that we become strong enough to travel the road of life.

It's so hard to get to a place where you can completely entrust your life to God, but once you do you find that nothing else compares to it. Finding that place where you can simply rest is a beautiful place. Not too many people find it. We get so caught up in how to live life that we forget how to simply just be in life. Jim Elliott once said, "Wherever you are, be all there." His story is remarkable, as he decided to go on the mission field to a place that was unwilling to hear about who God was. He went and gave his life for it. He went with all his heart; he didn't leave anything behind. He exhibited a good example of how

Find rest, O my soul, in God alone; my hope comes from him.
— Psalm 62:5

COMMIT

to be completely where you are. This is what we need to do. Find that place where you can simply rest in God and be all there.

Then we talked about delighting ourselves in God. This often seems like an easier thing to do, but maybe it's because we don't look at the scripture in context. We need to see that delighting ourselves in God means giving ourselves to Him fully. Letting Him be number one, so that every desire can first line up with what He wants for our lives. Only then can we find ourselves in a place where our desires' flow for Him is unending. Once we surrender our hearts to Him and find that He is our sole companion, then we are able to see how He meets each and every desire within our hearts.

Now, we get to experience a new part of the journey. We haven't been here yet, but it's a great place to be. Psalm 37:5 says, "Commit your way to the Lord; trust in Him and He will do this…" Commit is such a powerful word. People commit themselves to all kinds of things without knowing the implications of their commitment. We commit ourselves to friendships, to relationships, to children, to our jobs, to our families, to our ministries, etc. We commit ourselves in so many areas. Sometimes we become drained because every area decides to draw from us at the same time.

But your hearts must be fully committed to the Lord our God, to live by his decrees and obey his commands, as at this time.
—1 Kings 8:61

So if we know that we commit ourselves to too many things, why do we continue to do so? Often we do this because we long for assurance that we are doing the right thing. I know I certainly do. I long to know that I am fulfilling a great plan for God. That I am on my way to seeing my destiny come about. But in the midst of over committing myself, I lose sight of the one person to Whom I'm supposed to be completely committed. The

COMMIT

only one who deserves my complete commitment is God. He's the only One who will follow through on His end of the bargain. He will never lose track.

Then there are other times when people think that they can trust and delight in God, but nothing else needs to be done. Or maybe they do get to the commitment part but don't know how to completely follow through on it. Waylon B. Moore once said, "Many of you have put a period mark by your commitment. You need to erase that period and let God lead you further now!" Let's erase the period and find out what God wants to do next in our commitment to Him. It's going to be an adventure. Trust me. God never does anything without a little adventure involved. Feel free to take out your eraser. Erase the end, and let's start again. Let's get to the rest of the story.

First, look at commitment as a compass. A compass guides your way to wherever you need to go. It is not the end result, but it is a means by which to get to the end result. I've looked at Psalm 37:3–6 as my compass throughout life because no matter where I am in life, it has led me to the next part of my journey. Our church has a saying that goes into our weekly newsletter, "Aligning Our Hearts to True North." What does it mean to align our hearts to True North? Well, let's find out.

A compass shows you where the north is and you can choose to follow the path that leads north or you can find yourself gallivanting off onto different side trails. Once you find your way north, what do you do next? I think there are

The plans of the diligent lead to profit as surely as haste leads to poverty.

—Proverbs 21:5

some different things that we can do to keep our hearts going north. Some of which are meditating on God's Word, praying, listening to God, and following through on what He asks of us. The first thing I will ask of you is that you create small goals. It is said that people who make lists are more productive than people who don't. Why do you think that is? I think it's because they know what they want to do then they set their minds to accomplish it. We need to set goals in our lives so that we have something to go after.

Another way of putting this is thinking about what we sow. Meaning what are we putting into the ground for growth. Are we putting the things of God into our lives so that we reap His goodness and His character within us? The Bible says,

> ***A man reaps what he sows. The one who sows to please his sinful nature, from that nature will reap destruction; the one who sows to please the Spirit, from the Spirit will reap eternal life. Let us not become weary in doing good, for at the proper time we will reap a harvest if we do not give up.***
>
> —Galatians 6:7–9

I look at sowing as a way to commit to our goals. We will never see a harvest on our goals if we do not at first commit to sow them. One saying that has become quite popular is . . .

> ***Sow a thought, and you reap an act.***
> ***Sow an act and you reap a habit.***
> ***Sow a habit, and you reap a character.***
> ***Sow a character and you reap a destiny.***
>
> —Charles Reade

Our goals will not be accomplished just because we decide to have them. No, we need to commit to seeing them through. Let the compass of life guide you to True North. Find your direction in God and don't give it up for anything. In the next few chapters we will find out how to really use this compass. What can we do to be completely committed

COMMIT

to following God? Don't get lost in the shuffle. Find your niche and go with it. Let God show you how He wants to help you accomplish your goals for His sake. Only then can you truly find satisfaction in all that you reap.

The man who reads but one book, and that book his Bible, and then meditates much upon it, will be a better scholar in Christ's school than he who merely reads hundreds of books, and meditates not at all.

—Charles Spurgeon

Chapter 13
PLAN OF ACTION

One of the tools we pick up along our way is reflection on God's Word. We need to read it and let it sink into the very depths of our soul. We need to let God use it to bring about a change in us. How can you know that you are off-course if you don't know what the Word says? It's easy to read the Bible on a daily basis, but sometimes it's hard to apply it to our lives. There are three steps within meditation: first, thinking over what you have read and pondering it in your heart; second, setting up a plan on how to follow through on what you have read; and third, taking action on what you have read. What good is pondering, if you have no intention of developing a plan of action? And what good is a plan of action, if you have no intention of following through on it?

Do not merely listen to the word, and so deceive yourselves. Do what it says.

— James 1:22

Let's take a simple passage in the Bible and break it down, find out how it applies to your life, and learn how to further live by God's Word. Romans 12:2 says, "Do not conform any longer to the pattern of this world, but be transformed by the renewing of your mind. Then you can test and prove what God's will is—His good, pleasing, and perfect will."

COMMIT

In thinking over this passage, I took my time. I let things sink in and tried to find out what it meant for me. One thing I came to know is how essential this passage of scripture is for the day in which we live. Society tries to create an environment that will influence us to do as it wills and tempt us away from God's will for our lives. This verse says that we are not to conform to the pattern of this world; we're not to give into society's wishes for us. Instead, we need to let God transform our minds for His sake. How do we transform our minds in a society that is constantly trying to fill our heads with junk? The passage says we do this by renewing our minds. We renew our minds by pondering God's Word, letting it sink in, and letting it take effect in our lives. Only then can we truly fathom what His will is for us and how to live by it.

What is conformity to the world? Pastor Drew Worthen puts it this way,

> ***Conformity to the world is evil behavior which is nothing more complicated than a sinful, rebellious attitude of the heart toward our Creator, which manifests itself in selfishness as it seeks to please self and turn away from God's truth and will found in Christ.***

It is basically conforming to what the world would desire from us, instead of desiring what God wants in our lives. We take the time to transform this pattern by following the next step.

The next step is laid out in your plan of action. Every sports team has many plans of action. They have signals and names for things, no matter which sport it is. They know how to work together because they have learned the

The world and its desires pass away, but the man who does the will of God lives forever.
— 1 John 2:17

plans for action and have learned to follow through on them. We need to come up with plans of action for our own lives. Why should we

COMMIT

come up with anything less than what is required of a football team or baseball team? God wants to be involved in the plan of action for our lives so that we can work as a team with Him alone.

My first plan of action with this verse was to simply memorize it. I knew that I needed to put it in my hard drive, so that I could practice it on a daily basis. Then I needed to find out what were some of the ways that I was conforming to the ways of the world. I can list a few for you: gossip, unforgiveness, bitterness, selfishness, and worry. The list could go on, but thankfully throughout my time of following God the list is becoming shorter. I'm learning to let Him determine each step.

Another plan of action that I needed to come up with was how I was going to transform my mind. I looked at the things that were on my worldly list and decided I needed to come up with a similar list to battle them. This list would include scripture and what to do if I fell into the trap of conformity to the world. The next step in my action plan was to decide how I was going to let God show me His will. I wanted to know how to test it and how to follow through on it.

After coming up with my plan of action, I decided to put it to the test. After all, what's a good theory if you never follow through on it with action? The first thing I did was memorize the verse. I placed it on a note card and carried it with me everywhere, so I could pull it out and apply it to my memory. After memorizing it, I filed the note card away.

Then I came up with my list of things that I was doing wrong. That's when things got tough. I really dislike looking at those dark areas of my life, but I know that I can never get passed them if I don't face them. So the pen and paper came out. I listed everything that God put on my heart. I didn't want anything left in me that wasn't conforming to only His likeness.

COMMIT

Once I came up with this list, I had to find out how to counteract these things inside of me that I did not like to see. I prayed that God would reveal to me all of these things inside my life and help me to place them in His hands. It was tough. I remember going through a period of time where it seemed like I constantly had to make things right because my mouth would open before my heart could stop it. I had to go back to many people and express that I was sorry for things that I had done and even share the things they did not know about. It was tough, but it was good because it was a cleansing process. I was letting God take over and slowly relinquishing any say I had in it.

I know that nothing good lives in me, that is, in my sinful nature. For I have the desire to do what is good, but I cannot carry it out.
— Romans 7:18

Then the good list came out—the list of scripture to battle the list of worldly conformities. I came up with a scripture for everything that was revealing darkness inside of me. Soon I could see that God was shining His light through my broken pieces. Jesus said,

> **You are the light of the world. A city on a hill cannot be hidden. Neither do people light a lamp and put it under a bowl. Instead, they put it on its stand, and it gives light to everyone in the house. In the same way, let your light shine before men, that they may see your good deeds and praise your Father in Heaven.**
> —Matthew 5:14–16

I came to see that my reflection of God was a light on a hill. I can't hide who I am. People of the world will constantly use a measuring stick to see if we are who we say we are. The only thing I have to say to this is that the measure of a man is not how tall he stands, but how fully his heart is dedicated to God. So the next time someone takes

COMMIT

out their measuring stick to measure how tall you are, remember you are a workmanship of the King. Shine His light. Let people see who He is through you. Don't let measurement scare you off. We will never measure up to our full potential on this earth; we will only attain that in Heaven. We need to use the time on this earth to point people to Jesus. Help them remember that you are just trying to be a mirror image of what you find in your Father. You don't have all the answers and you never will, but you do know the One who does. Count on Him!

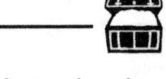

But the Lord said to Samuel, "Do not look at his appearance or at his physical stature, because I have refused him. For the Lord does not see as man sees; for man looks at the outward appearance, but the Lord looks at the heart."
— 1 Samuel 16:7 (NKJV)

Those are the steps. This is just one passage of scripture that can make a huge impact in your life. There are many more, and to each one of them I would say, ponder it, let it sink into the depth of your soul, and then set aside a plan of action. How are you going to follow through on what you see in Scripture? Most importantly, go for it! Go for the goal line. See what you can do and do it. Let God reveal to you your full potential in Him and don't settle for anything less than His best. That's what He is offering you.

In prayer, it is better to have heart without words, than words without heart. Prayer will make a man cease from sin, or sin entice a man to cease from prayer. The spirit of prayer is more precious than treasures of gold and silver. Pray often, for prayer is a shield to the soul, a sacrifice to God, and a scourge for Satan.

—John Bunyan

Chapter 14
LET'S TALK

If you started this chapter without first reading the quote, then I encourage you to go back and look it over. We are going to search the Bible for the answer on how to pray. Prayer is an essential thing; a life without it is a life without communication. God is the Great Communicator, and He gave us words to speak to express ourselves to Him. There is no magic in how you say a prayer or the words that you use in it. The magic does not come from a formula. Everyone is looking for a way to pray. There are many different types of prayers and I know that I am only going to scratch the surface when it comes to this topic. There are many, many books written that can help you further your prayer life. This book is simply sharing where you can start when it comes to prayer.

First and foremost, please empty your mind of all the negative associations you might have when it comes to prayer. Let's make it simple again, and find out what it means to really pray. Let's find out what it means to simply

Continue earnestly in prayer, being vigilant in it with thanksgiving.
— Colossians 4:2 (NKJV)

communicate with the One who made you. Yes, let's talk with God. Let's enjoy Him in a new way and see prayer as a building block when it comes to our relationship with Him. He's not looking for anything

COMMIT

spectacular when it comes to the form of prayer you use. He's simply searching for your heart. He wants you to just get real with Him. Open up your soul; express to Him what you are feeling and what you desire.

There is an email that has circled through my in-box a few times. This story is about a man who does not know how to pray. His story begins with a pastor coming to see him on his deathbed. His daughter had made a request for the pastor to come see him. While the pastor was there, he saw an empty chair next to the bed and assumed that the man must have known he was coming. So he asked the man and the man simply shared this story...

"All of my life I have never known how to pray. At church I used to hear the pastor talk about prayer, but it went right over my head. I abandoned any attempt at prayer until one day, four years ago, my best friend said to me, 'Johnny, prayer is just a simple matter of having a conversation with Jesus. Here is what I suggest. Sit down in a chair; place an empty chair in front of you, and in faith see Jesus on the chair. It's not spooky because Jesus promised,

"I will be with you always." Then just speak to Him in the same way you're doing with me right now.'"

The old man went on to share how he did exactly that. He got to a point that he enjoyed it so much, that he started to do it a couple of hours every day. So many times we look at prayer as drudgery and

Then you will call upon me and come and pray to me, and I will listen to you.

— Jeremiah 29:12

don't know how we can possibly make it through even a few minutes of it. But the truth of the matter is that prayer is simply a conversation with God. An utterance of what is inside of our heart.

COMMIT

Real prayer is life creating and life changing. To pray is to change. Prayer is the central avenue God uses to transform us. If we are unwilling to change, we will abandon prayer ... When we pray God slowly and graciously reveals to us our hiding places and sets us free from them ... In prayer, real prayer, we begin to think God's thoughts after Him, to desire what He desires, to love the things He loves ... All who have walked with God have viewed prayer as the main business of their lives ... For those explorers in the frontiers of faith, prayer was no little habit tacked onto the periphery of their lives—it was their lives.
—Richard Foster, from Celebration of Discipline

Prayer does not have to be a structured thing. Yes, it should be a part of the structure of our lives, but prayer itself does not have to come in only one form. Your prayer life will be different than my prayer life, and that's the way it should be. God wants you to express your heart to Him. What is it that you would like to say to Him? Can you take the time to imagine that He is right before you and just wants to have a conversation with you? Try it! You might be surprised at how much easier praying becomes when you are focusing on praying to an actual person. He is someone who truly cares about every part of you.

Another aspect of prayer is making it a part of your daily life. Some people set aside certain times of the day to devote to prayer and that can be a good thing. For me, I like to see myself in a constant conversation with God all day long. Many times throughout the day something will come to mind, and I simply lift it up to God. I stop where I am, focus on Him, and express what's on my heart. You can do the same thing. God goes everywhere you go; you don't have to be in a certain place at a certain time to just talk to your Father. He is always ready to listen to your prayers.

COMMIT

Another important thing to remember is that coming to God with a clean heart will help you be better focused on the details you need to pray about. If there is unforgiveness in your heart or bitterness towards someone, you might find it hard to really get into a prayer time. So start by cleansing yourself of things that

And when you stand praying, if you hold anything against anyone, forgive him, so that your Father in heaven may forgive you your sins.

— Mark 11:25

don't belong in you. Psalm 51:10 says, "Create in me a pure heart, O God, and place a steadfast spirit within me." Start with a clean slate; offer to God all those things inside of you that just don't belong.

I remember one time when God gave me an opportunity to pray with a coworker. She was going through some tough times, and I asked her if it would be okay for me to pray with her. I started to pray God's heart for her, I prayed that He would show her how much He loved her and that He would become more real to her. Honestly, I really don't even remember everything that I prayed, but I know that I was praying my heart out for her. When I finished, I opened my eyes and looked at her. She had tears in her eyes and said, "You pray like you know God."

That touched me more than I can even begin to explain to you. I've had the privilege to know God since I was a young girl. I've opened myself up to Him in a way that is real. I pray like I know Him because I do know Him and I know that He knows me. Prayer is a great gift from God. Do you pray like you know God? Remember that you are praying to someone who knows your heart. There are no secrets where God is concerned. He knows you better than you will ever know yourself. You can come to know Him in better ways by simply conversing with Him on a daily basis, moment by moment.

COMMIT

I want to share one more story with you about prayer. About seven years ago when I was in college, I was a part of a ministry called the Brooklyn Gospel Team. As a team, we would head into Brooklyn every Friday night to simply get to know the people around that area. The area I was committed to was called Sunset Park. God did many things in this park that only He deserves the praise for. One encounter I had there was very special to me because once again God used prayer to break through someone's walls and reveal Himself to her.

I remember seeing this girl walking through the park, looking as lost as she could possibly be. I don't mean lost like she didn't know how to find her way home. I mean lost like she was missing something inside. I went up to her and expressed how much God truly loved her. That's when it happened. She broke, her walls came down and the tears started to fall. God was starting something new in her life. She had been raised in the Christian faith but walked away from it and now was searching for her way back. We spent quite a bit of time sitting on a bench in the park; I listened to her express her heart, and then I let her know that I would be praying for her.

Later that week, I received a letter in the mail from her. She told me how thankful she was for that night and how much she really needed to know God's love at that point and time. The second page of her letter is what struck me the most as it says,

> ***I just need your prayer. Tell the Lord to help me. I need Him, I love Him. Tell Him to remember me. I'm not a bad person, I was just stubborn. But please to enter my life quickly because the evilness is trying to destroy me and He cannot permit that because I'm His child. Sarah, I hope I'm not asking too much. But I really need some healing.***

COMMIT

She was not asking too much at all. I was so willing to pray for her, but even more than that I wanted her to know that she could talk to God too. It doesn't matter where you are or what you have done. God has not turned His back on you. You can come running home to Him any time you want to. He's waiting for you with open arms and is willing to hear your prayers. You don't need to go through a third party to get your prayers answered. Hebrews 10:22 says,

> **Let us draw near to God with a sincere heart in full assurance of faith, having our hearts sprinkled to cleanse us from a guilty conscience and having our bodies washed with pure water. Let us hold unswervingly to the hope we profess, for He who promised is faithful.**

We serve a faithful God who is faithful to us, even when we are unfaithful to Him. Don't think for a moment that God is not waiting for you to just draw near to Him. Come close … hear His heart of love beating for you!

If My people who are called by My name will humble themselves, and pray and seek My face, and turn from their wicked ways, then I will hear from heaven, and will forgive their sin and heal their land.

— 2 Chronicles 7:14 (NKJV)

PRAY WITHOUT CEASING

If you lower the ambient noise of your life and listen expectantly for those whispers of God, your ears will hear them. And when you follow their lead, your world will be rocked.

—Bill Hybels

Chapter 15
LETTING GOD SPEAK

What does it mean to let God speak? In what ways can we hear His voice? Will He speak to me? Are these some of your questions? Well, let me start out by telling you that you are not alone. Thousands upon thousands of people long to hear God's voice for direction in their lives. Some think they have mastered the skill of hearing God's voice and others don't know where to start. No matter where you are, I'm hoping this chapter will enrich your awareness of those times that God is speaking directly to your heart. May you hear Him in the whisper, as well as in the thunder during a storm. I hope you learn that God speaks to us through various ways. He longs to speak to you. Will you stop and listen, if even for a moment?

You will seek me and find me when you seek me with all your heart.

— Jeremiah 29:13

Here is a story about a man who stopped to listen. He was looking for God to speak in many different ways, but when it came right down to it God simply spoke in a whisper. His name was Elijah.

The Lord said [to Elijah], "Go out and stand on the mountain in the presence of the Lord, for the Lord is about to pass by." Then a

COMMIT

great and powerful wind tore the mountains apart and shattered the rocks before the Lord, but the Lord was not in the wind. After the wind there was an earthquake, but the Lord was not in the earthquake. After the earthquake came a fire, but the Lord was not in the fire. And after the fire came a gentle whisper ...

—1 Kings 19:11–12

Did you follow this story? Did you see all the ways that we in our lives tend to look for God to speak? We want it to be easy. We want to hear Him the way we want to hear Him, so that we will be unable to deny that He is truly speaking. Well, God doesn't always work that way. I'm not saying there won't be times that God speaks in a loud voice, but I will tell you that most often it will be through a whisper. Can you hear His whisper? To hear a whisper, you must stop the spinning world around you and just focus on God.

Realize that as powerful as the wind can be, it might not contain the answer. It will sweep by us, but it may just be the wind taking its course. Then there are those earthquakes and those fires; better known as the huge experiences with God where He speaks in a loud resounding voice through churches, conferences, friends, family members, and spiritual leaders. Yes, God can and does at times speak through these things, but more often than not, it's through a simple whisper.

We need to step back from the daily activity that tries to run our lives and humbly listen to an active God who is trying so desperately to speak to us. Find Him in the whisper. You may be saying, "Okay great, find Him in the whisper ... What does that mean? I have no idea what you are talking about." Well, I'm glad that you haven't been clued in on this yet because I have a special opportunity to show you some of the ways in which God might speak to you.

COMMIT

He speaks in many different ways. I have heard God speak to me most strongly through nature, but there are times He uses movies, music, art, books, quotes, etc. God can and will do anything to get your attention, but will you stop long enough to listen. It's important to step away from the hustle and bustle of life at times and just wait on God. Throughout my life there have been different places where I can go and hear God so much easier because all the distractions of a busy world do not exist there.

Wait for the Lord; be strong and take heart and wait for the Lord.
— Psalm 27:14

While I was in college, I would climb the hill behind our school and sit on a rock far up off the trail. Sometimes I would bring a journal, other times I would bring worship music to listen to, and still other times I would bring nothing. I just wanted to hear God. I would climb to my rock, my place of refuge and there I would quiet my soul before God. It was me, the birds, the squirrels, and God. It was great! Sometimes, I wouldn't say anything. I would just lay there looking up at the sky and admire all that God had made. Other times, I would be sitting journaling my heart away. And still other times, I would sing out all that was on my heart.

It didn't matter what I did up there because no one was there to think that I was crazy. It was just me and God. I started to look forward to those times every weekend because it was then that I got to go on a special date with God. It was an opportunity to spend time with just Him, in our special place. Once in a while, I would bring a journal in which I wrote letters to my future husband. I was writing away when I became suddenly distracted by a squirrel.

COMMIT

In my journal I wrote these words,

> *I have to tell you about this squirrel that I am watching right now. It seems to be storing acorns in its mouth and then hiding them. Nature is so much more fun to watch than television. This squirrel definitely has a plan and is preparing for the winter. This little guy burrows underneath the leaves to hide his acorns. It's not even the acorn, but the nut inside of it. He seems to know exactly what he's doing and he's not getting bored. It's hard to believe that God knew that's what squirrels would do even before He created them. God is so strategic, even the little details matter to Him. It's cool to think if He cares that much about a squirrel to implant these survival techniques, than how much more must He care for me. He definitely has all the details planned out.*

I wrote these words in December of 1998. At that time, I was going through some whirlwind events with my family. I was over a thousand miles away from them, and I knew that they were going through some tough times. I wanted to be there for them, but I couldn't be. I needed to know that God was taking care of them, and I can tell you that I felt He was when I walked away from my rock that day. You see, I learned that God cares so much more about me and my family than a silly little squirrel. His plans for us are not delayed by anything; He is constantly at work within every circumstance that surrounds our lives. He always shows up on time!

But if from there you seek the Lord your God, you will find him if you look for him with all your heart and with all your soul.
— Deuteronomy 4:29

"And we know that in all things God works for the good of those who love Him, who have been called according to His purpose" (Romans 8:28). At the time that this whirlwind hit, I saw nothing good coming

COMMIT

out of it, but I decided to focus on this scripture knowing that God had given me a promise through these words and I could hang on tight to this promise. Well, later after many bumpy roads, God did bring about good. It wasn't exactly how I wanted to see it, but it was exactly as it should be. Today my testimony of God's love is expanded and my family is strong in ways that they couldn't have been without these experiences.

Another way that God can speak to you is through the media environment. Every time I go to a movie, I try to find something in it that applies to my life. Watching a movie takes about two hours out of my life. Sometimes it takes even more time. I want to make sure that time is well spent, so in order to do that I look for ways to see God in the movie.

I remember expressing this to a friend one time and now he blames me for not ever being able to watch a movie without seeing something more behind it. I don't mind being blamed for that. The treasure of God can be found so strongly in a movie. Sure, that's not the intention of most movie directors, but God is capable of directing them in ways that they do not even comprehend.

One movie that has spoken volumes into my life lately is *The Notebook*. This is a remarkable story about an older man who loves his wife so much that he reads a journal to her every single day. She has Alzheimer's and is unable to remember who he is, but he continues to come back to her day after day to read the story of their love. It's such a true picture of God's love. God continuously reminds us of how He sent His Son to die on the cross for us. There are days that we forget and sometimes days that we don't even acknowledge His existence, yet He continues to come back to read the story of His love for us.

COMMIT

The movie, *The Notebook*, expresses love from a human perspective, but when you amplify it by a thousand times you can see God's portrayal of love towards us. John 3:16–17 says,

> ***For God so loved the world that He gave His one and only Son, that whoever believes in Him shall not perish but have eternal life. For God did not send His Son into the world to condemn the world, but to save the world through Him.***

Do you hear how much God loves you through this? Over and over again in history, God's people have turned away, but God continues to remain steady. He is ever constant in our lives, giving up hope that we will open our eyes to see His love in a bigger way.

The whole Bible is God's love story to you. It's right at your fingertips. Open it up, see what God wrote to you and realize that His love for you cannot be measured. Let Him speak through His Word. Find time to delve into it and see that He had you in mind even when He was writing it.

The Lord is good to those whose hope is in him, to the one who seeks him; it is good to wait quietly for the salvation of the Lord.
— Lamentations 3:25-26

Other ways to hear from God are through music, art, quotes, books, etc. I just want to quickly glance at these things because honestly you will never truly know what it's like to hear God, until you stop to listen. I can't do that for you. I wish I could. I wish I could stop you in your tracks and phase out the world for you, so you could simply hear His voice. But I can't. You are the one that needs to stop to hear the Father's voice.

COMMIT

One way to use music is to find a song that really ministers to your heart and let it play over and over again. Let the words sink into your soul and let them minister His healing in your life. Listen to what He has to say. One song that has done a tremendous work in me was written by Darrell Evans. The words of it are a soothing balm for my aches and pains. Here is the chorus from the song "I Know," on the Freedom album:

But I know that your love is unfailing
O I know your grace is so amazing
O I know even though my faith be shaken
O I still know that I'll never be forsaken
'Cause You're always faithful

I can tell you that my copy of this song is almost worn out because of the extensive amount of times that I have listened to this song. Don't forget that God is faithful. He will see you through your darkest hour. Let Him speak to you through the music that you listen to. Hear His sweet voice. Walk away from the song with assurance that God is at work in you.

Art is also a very popular way to see God. Some people draw, others simply enjoy viewing the work of artists. Either way, if you take the time to listen, you can hear God speak.

The next time you view a painting or drawing, ask God what He would like you to glean from it. Allow Him to open your eyes to see the work that is portrayed in each masterpiece.

The last two things that I will briefly share about are the ways you can hear from God through books and quotes. There are books out there on every possible subject you can imagine. Everyone has wisdom in

COMMIT

different areas. Feel free to pick up a book on prayer, fasting, devotions, etc. If you have questions in a certain area, then read up on that area. Let God speak to you through the wisdom that He has placed in others around you. As Christians, we are to work as a team. Allow God to use different books to show you who He is in an even clearer way.

I talk about quotes and how they too can speak to us of who God is and what He is trying to say to us. I say this because many times there will be a quote in a movie or a sermon or in something someone is saying that speaks to me. Quotes come in various forms and can be applied to our lives in various ways. "But seek first His kingdom and His righteousness, and all these things will be given to you as well." (Matthew 6:33) Seek God first; everything else will fall into place when you simply surrender your life to the work of His hands.

Seek ye First the Kingdom of God

The more of God's Word you know and love, the more of God's Spirit you will experience.

—John Piper

Chapter 16
STRETCH THOSE LEGS

*L*et's get the blood pumping and start moving to the rhythm of a new beat. A beat that has been set in place through the words that God has spoken to your heart. We see that God can speak through His Word, His world, His people, and His resources. Now what do we do when we hear Him? Here's a hint: we don't just sit there! It's time to stretch our legs, get up, and walk out what God has shared with us.

Sometimes God will speak things that do not make any sense whatsoever, but that does not mean that it is any less legitimate. God has purpose behind everything that He asks you to do. Trust Him … He knows where He is going with this. Follow His steps!

By faith he left Egypt, not fearing the king's anger; he persevered because he saw him who is invisible.
— Hebrews 11:27

Take a moment to think of where we would be if some of the characters in the Bible decided not to take the giant step that God was asking them to take. In particular, think about Moses and all the strange things that God asked of him. Where would the Israelites have been if Moses didn't follow through on what God asked of him?

COMMIT

To start things out, God spoke to Moses through a burning bush. The Lord said,

> *I have indeed seen the misery of my people in Egypt. I have heard them crying out because of their slave drivers, and I am concerned about their suffering. So I have come down to rescue them from the hand of the Egyptians and to bring them up out of that land into a land flowing with milk and honey.*
> —Exodus 3:7–8

God was answering the cry of the Israelites and Moses was about to get the biggest call of his life. "So now, go, I am sending you to Pharaoh to bring my people the Israelites out of Egypt." (Exodus 3:10)

In the verses to follow, Moses has a conversation with God letting Him know how inadequate he is for the job. Have you ever had a conversation like this with God? I know I have. I've let Him know when I don't think I'm the best person for the job, but thankfully He doesn't let me stay in that frame of mind. And thankfully, Moses decided to stretch his legs by following through on what God had asked of him. He had no idea what was about to happen through his willingness to obey! Obedience, as you can see through Moses' story, doesn't always come easy, but it has its own reward when we follow through.

Let's follow this story a little bit. We can look into the different things that God asked of Moses and see how sometimes God asks these same things of us. Moses went against the crowd. He didn't swim with the other fish. In fact, I would say he was swimming in his own pool and walking to the beat of a different drum. He was doing precisely what we are called to do on a daily basis.

The first step Moses took was to simply go to Pharaoh and ask him to let God's people go. God had prepared Moses ahead of time, letting

COMMIT

him know that Pharaoh would not simply go along with this plan. There was going to be a war, but ultimately God was going to have the victory in every battle. After going to Pharaoh the first time, things looked grim. The Bible says,

> ***Moses returned to the Lord and said, "O Lord, why have you brought trouble upon this people? Is this why you sent me? Ever since I went to Pharaoh to speak in your name, he has brought trouble upon this people, and you have not rescued your people at all."***
>
> —Exodus 5:22–23

Sometimes life feels like this. God shows us that we must walk in a certain direction, but when we do we face opposition. Does this mean it's time to give up and turn back? Absolutely not! As God's people, we need to follow through on whatever He asks of us, even if the opposition looks fierce. Remember, the Promise Land is awaiting your arrival.

Moses continues to go back to ask Pharaoh to let his people go, but Pharaoh continued to take the same stance. He was relentless and unwilling to let them go. God directed Moses to perform a couple miracles. Both of these miracles are recorded in Exodus 7, but for the sake of time I will only focus on one of them.

The Lord said to Moses,

> ***Tell Aaron, "Take your staff and stretch out your hand over the waters of Egypt—over the streams and canals, over the ponds and all the reservoirs—and they will turn to blood. Blood will be everywhere in Egypt, even in the wooden buckets and stone jars."***
>
> —Exodus 7:19

COMMIT

Does this sound kind of crazy to you? It certainly does to me. But Moses and Aaron spent no time hesitating, they simply followed through.

There are times in our lives when God asks us to stretch out our hand and believe something will

And without faith it is impossible to please God, because anyone who comes to him must believe that he exists and that he rewards those who earnestly seek him.
— Hebrews 11:6

happen, even if rationale tells us otherwise. This is called an act of faith. 2 Corinthians 5:7 says, "We live by faith, not by sight." Remember this the next time God asks you to do something that doesn't line up with the logic in your head. You don't have to see something to believe it when it comes to God.

After a series of plagues and some devastating blows to the Egyptians, Pharaoh was finally ready to let the Israelites go.

During the night Pharaoh summoned Moses and Aaron and said, "Up! Leave my people, you and the Israelites! Go, worship the Lord as you have requested. Take your flocks and herds, as you have said, and go. And also bless me."
—Exodus 12:31–32

So the great Exodus began. The Israelites' freedom had finally been won. God didn't let them down. He followed through on His promise.

But the craziness did not end there and often it doesn't in our lives either. Just when we think we have made it past the safety point, something comes up. Don't get comfortable in God because the second you become comfortable you will not be ready for the things to come. God wants you to be hot or cold, not in between. We are not to live lukewarm lives; we are to be always on fire for Him, seeking His purpose in each moment of the day.

The Israelites' new found freedom would be tested soon enough. After Pharaoh and the Egyptians thought about things, they were unhappy with their decision. What would they do without their slaves? So they went after them. The Israelites were facing the sea, while their enemy was quickly approaching them from behind. It didn't take long for them to tremble with fear, but thankfully their leader was a God-fearing man.

> ***Then the Lord said to Moses, "Why are you crying out to me? Tell the Israelites to move on. Raise your staff and stretch out your hand over the sea to divide the water so that the Israelites can go through the sea on dry ground."***
>
> —Exodus 14:15–16

What do you think about this? Imagine yourself, standing before this great big sea that you can't even see the other side of and God tells you to "move on." I think I would be saying, "Are you kidding, God? Do You see this sea in front of me?" The truth of the matter is that God sees everything that lies in front of us, and trust me all mountains look like mole hills to him and every ocean is like a pond. He is able to do abundantly more than we could ever hope or imagine. God makes it sound so simple. He wants you to know that these kind of moments do exist in your life.

God has helped me see that He could have parted the Red Sea before the Israelites arrived, but they would have missed out on an opportunity to increase their faith in God. They had to come right to the edge of the sea, so their faith could be stretched. The next time you come to the sea, don't fret. God wants to part it right before your eyes. He wants to show you how much He loves and adores you.

COMMIT

God has asked me to do some pretty amazing things in life and many times I've wondered if He realizes what He is asking of me. Then I come to find out that yes, He knows exactly what He's asking of me.

He has a plan. His plan is bigger than the human mind can possibly understand. Moses and the Israelites continued to experience many more miracles throughout the book of Exodus. Each time they were amazed by God's hand of mercy on their lives. We too need to remember that God's hand of mercy is on our lives. The next time He tells you to do something that looks kind of crazy, don't fret, He'll walk you through it. He will be by your side the entire time. He wants you to experience the parting of the sea in your life too.

> ***"He is the Rock, his works are perfect, and all his ways are just. A faithful God who does no wrong, upright and just is he."***
> —Deuteronomy 32:4

Be Strong
Be Brave
Be fearless
you are never
alone

- Joshua 1:9 -

He is no fool who gives what he cannot keep to gain what he cannot lose.

—Jim Elliot

Chapter 17

WEARING THE RIGHT SHOE

The walk through this passage of Psalm 37 has been leading us to a wonderful place. I don't know if you noticed, but the last verse we covered kind of left us hanging. So what happens after you commit your heart to God? Well, He says, "He will make your righteousness shine like the dawn, the justice of your cause like the noonday sun" (Psalm 37:6).

This is the amazing part! It's like finding the pot of gold at the end of the rainbow. I liken this last part of the scripture passage to a treasure hunt. When I was younger, my mom used to set up clues for us that would lead us to a treasure. Each clue would tell us in a riddle how to get to the next place. Then the next place would have another riddle. We would follow these riddles, until we reached our destination where the treasure was hidden.

Now in this case the treasure could be a dollar, candy, cookies, small toys, etc. The treasure was always different. There were five kids, so mom kept us as busy as possible through her creative thinking. These treasure hunts were often one of the highlights of our week. I remember we would get so excited when we figured out the

For where your treasure is, there your heart will be also.
— Matthew 6:21 (NKJV)

RIGHTEOUSNESS

riddle. That was half the fun. The treasure at the end was great, but it wouldn't have been what it was had we not had to take the journey to get there.

God takes us on an adventure in Him to a place where treasure is waiting. I'm not talking about a small treasure. I'm talking about a treasure that cannot amount to what our eyes would want to make it. God has something big in store for each one of us. I remember watching the movie *Goonies* back in the 1980s. It was a great movie. A group of boys found a treasure map and decided that they were going to go on an adventure to find the X that marked where the treasure was on the map. In the very beginning of their journey, they came upon a wishing well filled with coins galore. All the boys were so excited and thought that they had found the true treasure.

Only one little guy believed there was more to the hunt. He determined in his heart to find the real treasure. He urged all the other boys to dig deep and find the courage to continue the hunt for the true treasure. So on they went. Though they faced many obstacles, they never gave up. And eventually they did find the treasure. They found a treasure ship filled with mounds and mounds of gold and jewels.

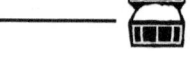

In My Father's house are many mansions; if it were not so, I would have told you. I go to prepare a place for you.
—John 14:2 (NKJV)

So many times in our own lives, we think we have found the treasure. We forget that God calls us onward. There is so much more in Him. We cannot begin to imagine all that He has in store for us. He has given us the map through His Word and through nature which speaks volumes of who He is. We need to set our hearts on doing His will, following through to the end, and refuse the wishing well mentality. God has much more in store for us my friend. Eternity awaits you and I!

RIGHTEOUSNESS

I remember one time when my old roommates and I decided to go visit their grandmother, my adopted grandmother, at the hospital. Her name was Mommom, and she loved to laugh. Often our moments would be called "Minnesota Experience." I was from Minnesota and all my experiences sure could make her laugh … Well, this day was unlike any other. I had been complaining to my roommates how my shoes just didn't feel right. I had just bought a new pair of sneakers, but for some reason they never seemed like the right size. I walked around in them for two weeks.

Well, I guess my roommates got tired of my complaining and asked to look at my shoes. Would you believe that one was an eight and a half and the other was a ten? No wonder I couldn't walk straight, I was wearing two different size shoes. Oh boy how we laughed and laughed at this. I kept trying to justify why I had never looked at the size of the shoes and how I didn't notice that big of a difference. It didn't matter what I said, they would just laugh all the more. And that is how I came to be known as the girl who provided a little "Minnesota Experience" for my adopted family.

Do you ever feel like you're walking in two different size shoes when it comes to this walk with God? It's difficult to do. Quite uncomfortable, that's for sure. Well, we walk in two different size shoes when we say one thing and do another. We walk in two different size shoes when we adapt to someone else's style of living instead of God's. I think we also find ourselves in the wrong shoes when we try to be more like the people around us instead of more like Jesus.

While Jesus was on this earth, He exhibited all that He wanted us to be. God has not asked us to trust Him without first providing

Jesus said to them, "My food is to do the will of Him who sent Me, and to finish His work."
—John 4:34 (NKJV)

RIGHTEOUSNESS

examples of His own Son putting His trust in the Father. We are not the only ones called to delight ourselves in God. Jesus was too! And commit? Oh my goodness … Jesus completed the ultimate act of commitment. He showed us what it is like to live out the very passage that I am trying to expound upon in this book. He lived it out so that we could see we would never be alone. He faced it all to show us that we could make it through anything if our dependence is solely on Him.

So what does it mean to have your righteousness shine like the noonday sun or the justice of your cause like the dawn? I know I can't adequately answer this because I have not seen Heaven yet. I can share with you my experience along the way, but it will not amount to all that Heaven has for you. So how does this last verse apply to life on earth? Well, let's explore this a little bit. Let's step into the right shoes, the ones we were meant to wear.

I think of how the world tries to shape us. It tries to tell us how to live, what to do, and when to do it. It is always sizing us up and letting us know what shoes to wear for what moments in life. Well, the shoes of this world do not fit. They are not comfortable. They don't belong on our feet. We are called to live for Christ in the depths of our hearts. We are called to live lives of righteousness for His name sake.

Matthew 5:6 says, "Blessed are those who hunger and thirst for righteousness, for they will be filled." Read it again, only more slowly this time. What fills you up? It says nothing about the world and its ways of filling us up. The emphasis is righteousness—hungering to be right with God. Only in this place will we find ourselves as an open vessel ready to be poured into. I love this verse because it expresses what the world so often tries to do

The world and its desires pass away, but the man who does the will of God lives forever.
—1 John 2:17

RIGHTEOUSNESS

through its media. The world wants to fill us up and make us feel fulfilled. They tell us money will do it. Clothing, a new car, a new hair style, or more friends will do it, but all of that just leaves you wanting more.

It's like taking a drink of soda. It leaves your mouth dry and thirsty for more. Why do you think that Jesus used water as a comparison so many times? "But whoever drinks the water I give him will never thirst. Indeed, the water I give him will become in him a spring of water welling up to eternal life." (John 4:14) Water quenches thirst. It is the only thing that leaves your mouth feeling satisfied. We have drinking fountains everywhere because at any moment you might be thirsty and one sip of water can get you through until you get to a place you can get more.

John Piper once said, "God is most glorified in us when we are most satisfied in Him." Do you find yourself wanting to be satisfied in Him? Do you see that He wants to be glorified through your life? I want you to take a trip with me down memory lane. Now I'm not talking about my memory lane where God has indeed created many great moments. I'm talking about the memory lane that Jesus walked when He was on this earth. Let's see how He lived out Psalm 37:3–6 and try to find out how we can truly follow His example. In the end, I think you will find the answer to the question of what it means to have your righteousness shine like the dawn and the justice of your cause like the noonday sun.

Never be afraid to trust an unknown future to a known God.

—Corrie Ten Boom

Chapter 18

A WALK THROUGH THE WOODS

*I*magine yourself entering a place where there is no direction on how to get out. Think of it as a big forest, and you see a place you can enter. You start to explore, looking at all the things that exist around you, and eventually you end up so deep in the woods that you can't possibly find your way out. You look left and you look right, but you forgot to leave the bread crumbs, so now you're searching for your way out. Many people in this world feel swallowed up by a huge forest. They are lost in the midst of its wondrous ways, searching for an exit.

The god of this age has blinded the minds of unbelievers, so that they cannot see the light of the gospel of the glory of Christ.
— 2 Corinthians 4:4

I remember a story of a little boy named David. He was someone I met through our Brooklyn Gospel Team. His heart was genuine, and he couldn't have been more than ten years old. Our team would try to take the kids from Brooklyn up to our college for one weekend every semester. It was a great time to get the kids out of the city, but you can imagine their eyes when they saw wilderness around them. They loved it. It was all new to them, and they were ready to explore.

RIGHTEOUSNESS

We once decided to take all the kids on a hike behind our school through the woods. We all had to partner up, and my partner was this little boy David. I remember walking through the woods and the look in his eyes was priceless. All that was around him mesmerized him. This was a whole new world to him, and his eyes shared a sparkle of excitement that could not be measured. He asked question after question. Where do trees come from? How did those big rocks get here? What makes the sun shine like that? So many simple questions asked from a heart that was pondering the significance of God's creation.

Little David was in awe of all that God had made around him. He saw the woods like God probably saw the world when He first created it. The most important question that David asked that day was "How are we going to find our way out?" Now remember, his hand was in mine the whole time. He wasn't going anywhere without me, but still he wondered … Is there an exit? Will we be able to find it?

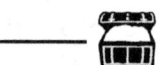

But Jesus called the little children to him and said, "Let the little children come to me, and do not hinder them, for the kingdom of God belongs to such as these. I tell you the truth, anyone who will not receive the kingdom of God like a little child will never enter it.
— Luke 18:16-17

Before I could answer his question, you could see the wheels turning in his head as he looked up to the sky and pointed with his hand, "You know the way out." His little heart conceived something that was so extreme that day. He recognized that no human could find their way out of a forest without God guiding them. The eyes of a child are so pure and so right. And I only hoped I could have the trust in God that I saw David have that day.

We often think that God doesn't know what it's like to be lost in a forest. He made it, so of course He knows His way out, but think of

RIGHTEOUSNESS

Jesus when He was led into the desert to fast for forty days. No, it wasn't a forest, but I bet He had some of the same feelings we have felt when lost in this big old world.

The Bible says He spent forty days fasting and at the end of them became very hungry. "The tempter came to Him and said, 'If you are the Son of God, tell these stones to become bread.' Jesus answered, 'It is written: Man does not live on bread alone, but on every word that comes from the mouth of God.'" (Matthew 4:3–4) Satan thought that he was going to get the best of Jesus because he was going to pick on Him during a weak moment, but Jesus placed His eyes on the Father. He put His trust in God, knowing that hunger would not kill Him.

Satan did not stop there. He continued to taunt Jesus and tried to plant seeds of doubt in Him by raising more questions. Jesus rebuked him every single time with God's Word. This is an example to me of how Jesus put His trust in God. He could have done any of the things that Satan was tempting Him to do, but He chose not to. He was showing us what can happen when we are fully surrendered to God and His work.

The last thing that Jesus says in this time of testing is, "Away from me, Satan! For it is written: 'Worship the Lord your God, and serve Him only.'" (Matthew 4:10) Jesus walked out of that desert fully intact. He never once gave in to the pack of lies that Satan was trying to sell Him. You see, the forest that we get lost in can be filled with lies that Satan wants us to believe, but we can know that we are not in it by ourselves. Just like David, we can look to the sky and point to God and say, "You know the way out." Yes, God knows the way out of your forest. He experienced the desert for you through His Son so that you would never have to feel like He doesn't understand you.

Jesus has been there. He has felt your pain. He too has had to put all of His trust in God, knowing that God's plan would succeed. Hebrews 4:15

RIGHTEOUSNESS

says, "For we do not have a high priest who is unable to sympathize with our weaknesses, but we have one who has been tempted in every way, just as we are—yet was without sin." He had to be without sin to be the perfect atonement for our sins.

He walked out of the desert with His eyes on God, knowing that He had just been through a test and had passed with flying colors. The next time you're walking through a deep dark forest and think that no one understands where you are, read the story of Jesus in the desert. You, my friend, are not alone. Jesus has walked every step that you could ever imagine walking and has promised to be there for you no matter what comes your way. He wants to guide you out of the forest into the beautiful arena of His grace and mercy.

But God demonstrates His own love toward us, in that while we were still sinners, Christ died for us.
— Romans 5:8 (NKJV)

Do you know that David and I finally did find our way out of the forest? We walked right out on the trail that God had provided, and when we got out, David looked again to the sky and said, "Thank You for helping us find our way out." When was the last time you thanked God for guiding you through your forest and, even more importantly, for helping you find the exit? That very same day David dedicated his life to God. He spoke a prayer and made Jesus the center of his life. He wanted to know that he didn't have to walk through life alone. That hike through the woods wasn't just an experience to see how nature works, but it was an experience to see who Jesus is and always will be.

The forty day fast in the desert is not the only time that Jesus had to trust God. There are numerous other times that He had to put His full trust in God. He was unwilling to accept any glory for anything; He continuously pointed people to His Father in Heaven.

RIGHTEOUSNESS

The reason my Father loves me is that I lay down my life—only to take it up again. No one takes it from me, but I lay it down of my own accord. I have authority to lay it down and authority to take it up again. This command I received from My Father.

—John 10:17–18

Jesus entrusted His life to God, even to the point of death. He did not hold back anything. Have you entrusted all of your life to God? Do you let Him determine your steps, even when you don't know what the outcome will be? God will never leave you empty handed. He has given you so much and is only asking that you simply trust Him. Let Him do His work in you.

"Trust in the Lord with all your heart and lean not on your own understanding; in all your ways acknowledge Him, and He will make your paths straight." (Proverbs 3:5–6) If you can, please take the time to commit this verse to memory. Let God remind you on a daily basis that you can entrust your heart to Him. Remember that even though you don't know what's to come it doesn't mean that it won't be good or profitable. For the Word says, "Every good and perfect gift is from above, coming down from the Father of heavenly lights, who does not change like shifting shadows." (James 1:17) God does not waiver. He is the same and always will be the same. You can trust Him to lead you through the forests and through the deserts of your life.

The climax of God's happiness is the delight He takes in the echoes of His excellence in the praises of His people.

—John Piper

Chapter 19

DELIGHTFUL VALUE

As a little girl, my favorite place to be was with my grandfather. In fact, whenever I see him he tells me how I would always cling to him. It didn't matter who else was around, I just wanted to be near my grandpa. There was something about him that drew me to him as a little girl and I have to say I never grew out of it. I still love going for walks with him, hand in hand, and hearing all about his stories. Some of them I have memorized, but I still ask to hear them again.

Another thing I love to do is put on music and dance around the kitchen with him. He still laughs at my jokes and always compliments me on my cooking. He is a true treasure in that all throughout my life he has found value in me; first as a little girl and now as a grown woman. I always enjoyed being delightful in his presence.

God calls us to this place every day. He longs to be the One in which we delight ourselves. In fact, Jesus shows us some very real examples of how important it

For great is the Lord and most worthy of praise; he is to be feared above all gods.

— Psalm 96:4

is to find delight in God. Once again, Jesus shows us that we have not been asked to do anything outside of what God had asked of Him.

RIGHTEOUSNESS

Jesus was constantly finding times away from the crowd to just be with His Father. He knew that He couldn't live without these times.

If Jesus, a perfectly divine man, needed times with God, how much more do we need to make sure that we spend time with God? Luke 4:42 says, "At daybreak Jesus went out to a solitary place." He sought time with God. He never depended on His own strength, but continuously went to be alone and gather strength from His Father. Jesus took time to delight in the presence of God. He did not let the busyness of life get to Him. Sure, He had plenty to do and many people desiring His attention, but He never forsook spending time with God. There isn't a single one of us that could ever claim to be busier than Jesus was when He was on this earth.

Another example where Jesus stole a moment away from the crowd is written about in Matthew 14:23, "After He had dismissed them, He went up on a mountainside by Himself to pray. When evening came, He was there alone." Jesus again exemplifies what we need to be doing on a daily basis. He shows us that we are incapable of being anything beyond God's strength within us.

Come, let us bow down in worship, let us kneel before the Lord our Maker; for he is our God and we are the people of his pasture, the flock under his care.
— Psalm 95:6-7

One last example that I will share with you is Luke 6:12, "One of those days Jesus went out to a mountainside to pray, and spent the night praying to God." Jesus saw the great significance in simply spending time in God's presence. He did not desire sleep over a desire to be with God. We too need to shape our lives like this. We need to get away from the crowd and the busyness of life, to just simply sit in God's

RIGHTEOUSNESS

presence. Find time to delight yourself in Him, as Jesus did and see the remarkable change that this will make in your own life.

I could list more times where Jesus got away to spend time with God, but I think you are already starting to get the point. I want to take the time to now show you how one woman gave of her very best for Jesus. She took time to delight herself in the Lord's presence, even at an incredible cost. This story has been retold many times but still has not lost its effect. Most people have heard the story of Mary and Martha and come to some kind of conclusion of which one they tend to be. In the next few pages, I want to outline the example of worship that Mary displayed at Jesus feet.

Martha was busy about the home, making sure the guests were happy and well fed. After all, she was opening her home up to a King. Not just any king, but the King of Kings. She wanted to make sure everything was perfect. Wouldn't you feel the same way if Jesus showed up at your door? Be honest! I think there is a little of Martha in all of us, but right now I want to expound upon Mary's delightful value in the Lord's sight.

Mary was not busy. She did not let herself be worried about tasks that needed to be done. Instead, she saw herself with this great opportunity to simply delight in the Lord's presence. She wanted to offer Him something good, something more than she could ever afford. You can imagine how she must have searched through the house to find a suitable gift for the King. Coming upon the perfect gift I'm sure she just lit up at the idea of how she could delight herself in the Lord.

Let's continue this story in John 12:3 where it says, "Mary took about a pint of pure nard, an expensive perfume; she poured it on Jesus' feet and wiped His feet with her hair. And the house was filled with the fragrance of the perfume." It is said that the perfume was worth about a year's wages in that time. One man looked on in pure disgust that

RIGHTEOUSNESS

such a waste of money would be poured out in such an extravagant act of worship. This one man, Judas Iscariot, was not concerned about the poor as he claimed to be in scripture. Instead, he was concerned about the money bag because he was a thief.

Jesus responds in a direct way saying, "Leave her alone. It was intended that she should save this perfume for the day of my burial. You will always have the poor among you, but you will not always have me." (John 12:7–8) Mark adds a little more to this story in his account, which states that what Mary did would be known. Jesus says, "I tell you the truth, wherever the gospel is preached throughout the world, what she has done will also be told, in memory of her." (Mark 14:9)

Ascribe to the LORD the glory and honor due His name; Bring an offering [of thanksgiving], and come before Him; Worship the LORD in the splendor of holiness.
— 1 Chronicles 16:29 (AMP)

What a story! Can you imagine being there in that moment when Mary broke the alabaster box that contained the most beautiful of fragrance and left a room stunned by her act of worship? I try to imagine it, but words can't seem to express all that I would feel in that moment. Think about all this. I mean break it down. Imagine having a guest of honor like Jesus in your home and searching for just the right way to express your gratitude to Him. She was looking for something that would stand out and leave a lasting aroma.

That day, the perfume spread throughout the home, and everyone could catch a whiff of its pleasurable scent. It could not be mistaken that perfume had been poured out; not sprinkled or given in tiny increments, but poured out. Do you have something valuable in your life that you can surrender to God in this way? Can you place your greatest value at

RIGHTEOUSNESS

His feet? I challenge you to find your place of worship in His presence. Truly delight in the One who gave it all for you that you might live an eternal life with Him in glory. Don't be satisfied with sprinkling a little of your valuable keepsakes on Him. No, give Him everything. Don't you think this is the very least that He deserves from us?

Do you remember the man who came to Jesus and asked what He must do to follow Him? He is known as the rich young ruler. He asked Jesus one day, "Teacher, what good thing must I do to get eternal life?" (Matthew 19:16) Do you know how Jesus responded? You might want to sit down for this one. Get yourself prepared because the rich young ruler was not prepared for the answer he received. Don't be fooled into believing a lie. Jesus is standing before this man expressing a great truth.

He starts by sharing that the man must follow the Ten Commandments. The man asks Him which ones. Jesus expresses to him that he must follow all of them. "All these I have kept," the young man said. "What do I still lack?" (Matthew 19:20) The big answer is coming. Are you ready for it? I hope so because in this answer you will find the truth that will lead you to the doors of eternal life.

Jesus answered, "If you want to be perfect, go, sell your possessions and give to the poor, and you will have treasure in heaven. Then come, follow me." (Matthew 19:21) Now Jesus wasn't asking anything more from him than He had asked from any of His other followers. He asked all of His disciples to give up their ways of life and simply follow Him. They responded with immediacy. They did not linger in their thoughts, for they knew Who was calling them forward, and they did not want to miss out on the opportunity of a lifetime.

However, the rich young ruler was quite different and did not respond in the same way. Scripture says, "When the young man heard this, he went away sad, because he had great wealth." (Matthew 19:22) We

RIGHTEOUSNESS

cannot be blinded by the wealth of this world as it too will fade. The only thing that lasts is eternity. Are you delighting yourself in God in a way that produces value? Do you surrender everything you have at His feet? There is a great cost to following Jesus, but the reward far exceeds the means by which we get there.

In this chapter we have explored a few elements of delight. You have seen how I delighted myself in my grandfather and, truth be known, I tend to delight myself in my heavenly Father in the same way. I often long to spend time with God and just bask in His presence. I enjoy my every encounter with Him and try my best to live each day fully for His purpose alone. The little girl that spent time clinging to her grandfather is the same grown woman who clings to her everlasting Father. God is everything to me and living a life for Him is the greatest adventure I could ever hope for. I daily wake up asking God to remove anything from me that is not of Him and in its place fill me up with Him. Nothing compares to being fully abandoned to God's purpose.

Yours, O LORD, is the greatness and the power and the glory and the victory and the majesty, indeed everything that is in the heavens and on the earth; Yours is the dominion and kingdom, O LORD, and You exalt Yourself as head over all.

— 1 Chronicles 29:11 (AMP)

Mary did not count the cost of the perfume she would pour over Jesus. Instead, she saw it as an act of worship for one who had called her to be so much more than she ever would have dreamed for herself. Jesus Himself spent time with God, which caused Him to delight in His Father.

Last but not least, we see what happens when we turn our eyes away from eternal treasure to simply get satisfaction from temporal riches. The young ruler walked away sad. He was looking for an answer, and Jesus gave it to him. Jesus gave him an opportunity to do such a great thing—to give up everything and follow Him. This is an experience that cannot compare to the greatest riches that this world will try to offer. So think about this the next time you see yourself asking God what it takes to follow Him. Take time to be ready for the answer. Don't ask Him, hoping that He will give you the answer you're looking for. Ask Him out of a desire to abandon anything that doesn't have to do with Him.

In closing this chapter I want to remind you of what Jesus says in Matthew 6:33, "But seek first His kingdom and His righteousness, and all these things will be given to you as well." There is no better place to be than at the feet of Jesus, seeking His purpose, and going after the reality of eternal life in Him. Don't miss the boat. Explore the options beyond this if you must, but don't forget to come back to the saving truth that Jesus is the One worthy of all our praise, honor, and glory. Find a way to give up what holds you back and enjoy a closer walk with God. Take time to be alone with Him. Jesus needed these times and so do you. I have needed them often in my life and know that I will continue to press on in them.

No horse gets anywhere until he is harnessed. No steam or gas ever drives anything until it is confined. No Niagara is ever turned into light and power until it is tunneled. No life ever grows great until it is focused, dedicated, disciplined.

—Harry Emerson Fosdick

Chapter 20
CALL TO COMMITMENT

I have never witnessed a greater call to commitment than the one that Jesus took on when He decided to be the sacrifice for our sins. His time spent in the garden of Gethsemane tells the story of a divine man who experienced human emotions. He knew everything He was called to do when He came to this earth. He never once doubted that He would follow through on all that God had asked of Him, but that does not mean that He didn't have heartache and pain-filled tears when facing death itself.

Again, He took the time to pray through His emotions. He told the disciples to sit and wait while He went to pray. Matthew 26:37 reports, "He took Peter and the two sons of Zebedee along with Him, and He began to be sorrowful and troubled." Did you catch this? He began to be sorrowful and troubled. A man filled with sorrow, not just any man, but a divine man. He was experiencing emotions to show us that we are not alone when we experience all kinds of emotion.

For we do not have a High Priest who is unable to sympathize and understand our weaknesses and temptations, but One who has been tempted [knowing exactly how it feels to be human] in every respect as we are, yet without [committing any] sin.
— Hebrews 4:15-16 (AMP)

RIGHTEOUSNESS

So here He is ready to enter another place of prayer. "Then He said to them, 'My soul is overwhelmed with sorrow to the point of death. Stay here and keep watch with me.'" (Matthew 26:38) Have you ever felt overwhelmed? I know I have. Jesus didn't allow Himself to stay in this overwhelming place. Instead, He sought out God. Let's learn something from this. Overwhelming feelings come and go, but God remains the same throughout it all. We are called to a place of prayer where we can find rest and refreshment in the Father.

"Going a little further, He fell with His face to the ground and prayed, 'My Father, if it is possible, may this cup be taken from me. Yet not as I will, but as You will.'" (Matthew 26:39) Are you catching this? Do you see how much Jesus cared about you as an individual that He took the time to experience sorrow for you? He was in the midst of praying and His disciples had fallen asleep. How many times do we fall asleep when we are called to pray? Do not let the enemy sneak in your back door and cause you to fall asleep when clearly God wants to use you to break through strongholds.

After admonishing the disciples for falling asleep, Jesus returned to His post. He expressed what was on His heart, "My Father, if it is not possible for this cup to be taken away unless I drink it, may your will be done." (Matthew 26:42) Again, He exclaimed that He wanted the will of His Father to be done, even if it contradicted what He was feeling inside. He was abandoned to the full work of God. Are you? Have you taken time to slow down and find out what God is asking of you? Trust me, there is a battle going on, and He is asking you to take on His full armor to fight against the darkness that wants to entangle you.

Jesus did not need to take the cup given to Him. It wasn't His to drink. It was your sin, my sin, the world's sin. He decided to drink it, not to bring glory to Himself, but to create a way by which we can be saved. He wanted to bridge the gap, so that we might know the Father, as Jesus knew Him. Jesus returned to His disciples one more time and found them sleeping.

RIGHTEOUSNESS

They were sleeping. The greatest act of violence in history was about to be played out, and they were sleeping through it. Wake up! You, me, all of us ... we need to wake up! Don't let this world disguise itself as a comfy little bed on which you can fall asleep. No! Decide for yourself right now that you will stand firm in God's Word. Practice what you see and let the love of the Lord linger in your heart.

Jesus decided to leave the disciples and go back to His praying post for a third time. He was dedicated.

This is how we know what love is: Jesus Christ laid down his life for us. And we ought to lay down our lives for our brothers.

— 1 John 3:16

You will never find a man in history more dedicated than He. He repeated the same thing He said in His first two prayers. He truly knew all that He would face in paying the price for our sins on the cross. He was willing to do it because the thought of you spending an eternity in Hell was more agonizing than the thought of bearing an inhumane death. Did you catch that? He did nothing for Himself. It was all for you and me. Don't let this moment slip by without expressing your gratitude for all that He did for you when He submitted to the cross.

We have seen commitment in many forms. Presidents have been committed to serve our country, missionaries have been committed to winning souls all over the world, men and women have been committed to marriage and parenthood, soldiers have been committed to fighting wars, firefighters have been committed to extinguishing fires, police officers have been committed to protecting law-abiding citizens, but no one will ever serve a greater commitment than Christ served on your behalf.

It is said that crucifixion on a cross is so cruel that they wouldn't dare consider it for Roman citizens. It was set aside for those who did heinous crimes and were clearly outside of the law. Yet, a man who was sinless in

RIGHTEOUSNESS

His very core took on an inhumane death so that we might experience life. Life! Death brings life. Amazing! The concept is hard to grasp, but I ask you to begin to explore all that Christ did when He walked the road of Calvary for you.

I know that every time I take communion, I become emotional. There are so many things I do on a daily basis that show that I am unworthy of such a love that has been poured out for me. I will never do anything to justify the love that God has so freely given to me through His Son Jesus Christ. The truth is you won't be able to either. So stop trying. You don't have to perform any more. You were never expected to pay your own debt. Jesus paid it on the cross. The penalty of your sins has been covered.

But God, being [so very] rich in mercy, because of His great and wonderful love with which He loved us, even when we were [spiritually] dead and separated from Him because of our sins, He made us [spiritually] alive together with Christ (for by His grace—His undeserved favor and mercy—you have been saved from God's judgment).
— Ephesians 2:4-5 (AMP)

So the next time you look at the word commitment and think of the busy days in your life filled with empty wishes to simply live out the American dream, rethink things. Remember what commitment stands for. You did not create it. I did not create it. God created it from the moment He created this great earth for us to enjoy. His great commitment to us has been proven to be faithful time and time again. You can read an immeasurable amount of stories of God's faithfulness to us throughout the Bible. Don't miss out. Dig deeper! Find your roots. Look at them from a different angle. Is there something blocking the growth of them? Ask God to remove those stones, so you can experience true freedom!

God never missed an opportunity to be faithful to His people and He certainly won't miss an opportunity to be faithful to you. He is the only One your heart can trust no matter what. He will come through for you!

RIGHTEOUSNESS

I want to share a journal entry with you from 2003. I keep a journal for my devotional times and in those times I record scripture that speaks to me. Then I pray it into my life because I really want to be someone who exhibits all that the Word exemplifies. This small insert from my journal will give you a deeper look at all I know I have been called to be in Christ, and I hope it challenges you to want that depth as well.

2 Timothy 4:2 says, "Preach the Word; be prepared in season and out of season; correct, rebuke, and encourage— with great patience and careful instruction." My prayer for this day after reading this verse was a simple response to a God who has given me so much more than I could ever have hoped for.

> *Lord, help me to be prepared in and out of season. I want to be the best that I can be for You. Help me to be a living example of who You are. I surrender my life to You and Your use. Help me to be energized by Your Word and thirsty to learn more. I abandon myself to You and pray that I may be used to correct, rebuke, and encourage others. May my instruction come from You, and may I constantly be aware of all that You want to do in and through me.*
>
> —Love, your daughter, Sarah

I place this insert here to let you know how easy it is to apply scripture to your life. On your own you will have a difficult time standing, but on God's Word you can stand firm. For the Bible does say, "If the Lord delights in a man's way, He makes his steps firm; though he stumble, he will not fall, for the Lord upholds him with His hand." (Psalm 37:23–24) May the Lord show you how firm your steps can be in Him and may you find yourself upheld by His hands. Walk in the light of His Word and let it illuminate the path before you.

*Your word is a lamp to my feet
and a light for my path.*
— Psalm 119:105

A chameleon lizard has the ability to change its color to blend into whatever atmosphere it is in. We are not to be 'chameleon Christians,' trying to blend in wherever we are, but are to be strikingly different.

—Author Unknown

Chapter 21
A Fresh Start

We have explored a great many things in this book and now we are at the greatest point. Psalm 37:6 says, "He will make your righteousness shine like the dawn, the justice of your cause like the noonday sun." We made it. We are at the top of this mountain. I want you to look down and enjoy the view. See what you have come through in the previous chapters and don't take a second of it for granted!

In a way, we have gone up and down some hills, trudged through some deep waters, experienced times in the desert, and now we are at the mountain peak. We have arrived at the place where X marks the spot. The treasure is here and has been waiting for you. Every book tries to have a great ending, but the greatest ending of all, in any book, is the one that expresses a new beginning, a fresh start. The Bible laid out a plan for us, and this book is simply to be supplemental reading to it. The Bible has so much more in it than I could ever give you in the pages of this book, but I'm hoping that through your time

> *You alone are the LORD; You have made heaven, the heaven of heavens, with all their host, the earth and everything on it, the seas and all that is in them, and You preserve them all. The host of heaven worships you.*
> — Nehemiah 9:6 (NKJV)

RIGHTEOUSNESS

of exploring you will have a desire to read God's Word. Go deeper. Find out what He wants to say to you.

So what does it mean to have your righteousness shine like the dawn? Can you imagine what that might look like? Have you ever seen a beautiful sunrise and just marveled at the colors in the sky? This is a masterpiece of art that you truly have to look at to experience the depth of its beauty. God wants to make your life shine like this. He wants to put purples, blues, and reds into your dawn, but first you need to give up the black areas.

Release to God anything that might be holding you back from letting Him take complete reign over your life. Let the darkness of your life fade into the sunset and in the morning God will make your life shine like the dawn. Yes, this is what He wants for you.

Some of you reading this book have already decided to follow God with all of your heart and that is great. I pray that this book will only further your growth in Him. May you find yourself desiring more of Him every day. Don't be satisfied with a status quo life.

On the same token, I pray that you will look at your salvation as a gift from God. Be ready to share that gift with others. John 3:16 is a very familiar verse to many of us, but stop and think about it for a moment. These words are powerful and they express the true gift that we have been given. If we

For it is by grace you have been saved, through faith--and this not from yourselves, it is the gift of God— not of works, so that no one can boast.
— Ephesians 2:8-9

appreciate the gift giver, we will want to express our gratitude by giving it to others. "For God so loved the world that He gave His one and only Son, that whoever believes in Him shall not perish but have everlasting life."

RIGHTEOUSNESS

The gift God has given you is eternal life. This gift is way too precious for you to keep it for yourself. Share it with a friend, with a family member, or with a fellow employee. Think about this beautiful gift just waiting to be unwrapped by someone new. Can you think of someone who would enjoy a perfect gift? Let me encourage you to remember that there will never be a more perfect gift than Christ's love which was poured out for us on the cross.

For those of you who have not experienced salvation through Jesus Christ, I want to share a little more with you. God's heart is huge for you. His love is abounding in immeasurable ways for you. He wants you to walk into His presence and experience the gift of His love. The death of Jesus on the cross was just the beginning of a new life for each one of us. John 19:28–30 says,

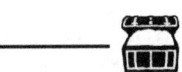

Therefore the Law has become our tutor to lead us to Christ, so that we may be justified by faith.
— Galatians 3:24 (NASB)

Later, knowing that all was now completed, and so that the Scripture would be fulfilled Jesus said, "I am thirsty." A jar of wine vinegar was there, so they soaked a sponge in it, put the sponge on a stalk of the hyssop plant, and lifted it to Jesus' lips. When He received the drink, Jesus said, "It is finished." With that, He bowed His head and gave up His spirit.

"*It is finished.*" These are the last words that Jesus spoke before giving Himself over to death. What was finished? The penalty for sin was finished. Jesus paid it in an agonizing way, but this was only the beginning of all that would be for you and me. Yes, the debt of sin was paid on the cross that day, and Jesus verbally expressed that this cost was finished. It's not to be mentioned again. Not in a way where

RIGHTEOUSNESS

we have to pay for it. It is only to be mentioned to lead you into an understanding of all that you lack, until you surrender yourself to the fullness of Jesus' death and resurrection.

Through this book, we have learned of three keys that can help us unlock the treasure box of God's love. We have learned to trust God with every step, to delight in Him with every action, and to commit every word to Him. This has led us to this place of righteousness. Do you want to be made right with God? Do you hunger for a life that is fulfilling? This kind of life can only be found in God. He is the one with all the answers. He holds nothing back from you, but instead gives it to you freely.

The Lord your God is in your midst, A Warrior who saves. He will rejoice over you with joy; He will be quiet in His love [making no mention of your past sins], He will rejoice over you with shouts of joy.
— Zephaniah 3:17 (AMP)

Come into His presence. Let Him embrace you with His Daddy arms and feel His love all around you. You are significant not for anything you can do in and of yourself. No, your significance and your worth come from God. He treasures you with all His heart. He sees you as a precious package and delights in your presence. Take the time to hand things over to Him. Don't let these moments slip by. Stop! Just stop and hear Him beckon you near. Listen to the words of His heart for you and start to sing a new song in Him.

God has called you by name. You are His child. You are a product of His workmanship. No one will ever find you more valuable than the One who created you. Simply decide to turn from your sins and turn your face towards Him. Let Him be Lord over your life and direct you in His ways. God desires to show you a whole new world and to be everything to you and for you in this new world. Get ready for a great adventure because, my friend, this is only the beginning. A fresh start awaits you.

Once you have decided to turn your life over to God, then follow Him by finding a community of fellow believers with whom you can relate. God wants you to know that you are part of a family. Find this family in a nearby church. Also, celebrate the life He has given you by reading His Word and finding more out about what He has done for you. Memorize portions of scripture to battle the lies that Satan will try to tell you. And find time to pray. Prayer is a great opportunity to simply express yourself to the One who already knows all your thoughts.

I pray this book will challenge you and help you see the difference of living a life deep in God's Word versus just living the status quo life. I'm telling you right now that nothing is more satisfying than living a life fully surrendered to God. I hope you find in Him the courage you need to take every new step. And I pray that your faith will be increased as you continue to walk in His ways. Remember this one last thing before we close the book: "Now faith is being sure of what we hope for and certain of what we do not see." (Hebrews 11:1)

Sometimes you will not see everything to understand your circumstances, but I can guarantee you that God is watching out for you from His throne. He doesn't take breaks from your life. He is fully involved and wants you to enjoy every moment. Take in a deep breath and let it out. Relax; enjoy the ride! It only gets better from here!

I can do all things through Christ

Study Guide

A Fresh Start
Chapter 1

*The purpose of Christianity is not to avoid difficulty,
but to produce a character adequate to
meet it when it comes. It does not make life easy;
rather it tries to make us great enough for life.*

— James L. Christensen

 Personal Reflection

1. Read Proverbs 3:5-6
   - Write down the images and thoughts that come to mind when you read the word "trust?" Describe the places that are the hardest for you to entrust to God.

- Write out Proverbs 3:5-6 in your own words and make it personal. For example,

  "I will trust in the Lord with all my heart and I choose not to lean on my own understanding; in all my ways I will acknowledge the Lord and lean on Him to make my paths straight."

2. Read Romans 8:28
   - Do you believe this? If so, reflect on why you believe it?
   - If not, what keeps you from believing it?

3. Read Psalm 20:7
   - In what are you putting your full trust? Be honest! Ask God and let Him show you.

Group Discussion

1. Read Psalm 37:3-6
   - Discuss your initial impressions when you read this verse.
   - What stands out to you and how can you apply it to your own life?

2. Read James 1:2-5
   - What test or trial are you facing right now?

   - How is God using your current circumstances to enhance your level of perseverance and strengthen your character?

3. Read Philippians 4:4-7
   - In what ways can you find joy in your circumstances and embrace the peace that God has for you?

HE SAID GO

Chapter 2

All that I have seen teaches me to trust the Creator for all I have not seen.

— Ralph Waldo Emerson

 Personal Reflection

1. Read Proverbs 16:9
   - What do you tend to do when God shows you something you don't want to do?

   - Will you let God determine your steps?

2. Read the song "It is Well" on page 23.
   - How can you relate to Horatio Spafford's story?

   - If you have the song on CD, listen to it and let God remind you that "It is well!"

3. Read Isaiah 40:28-31
   - Describe how your perspective on your current circumstances change when you take your eyes off of the storm and focus them on Christ?

Group Discussion

1. Read Exodus 33:12-14
   - Describe what makes it difficult for you to move in the direction God has for you when you can't see ahead.

   - Share a recent experience you had with this and how you overcame your insecurity in it.

2. Read Philippians 4:19
   - Please take the time to share a story of when God came through for you. Rejoice together in the work of God and let each story remind you of God's faithfulness.

NO NEED FOR EXTRAVAGANCE

Chapter 3

As a boy I toted two buckets of water, one balancing the other, grace works the same way. People see our 'Bucket of Trouble' easy enough. What they don't see is the 'Bucket of Grace' that balances out the 'Bucket of Troubles'.

— Ralph Waldo Emerson

 Personal Reflection

1. Read Matthew 11:28-30

    - Do you ever feel like your "Bucket of Troubles" is getting too full?

    - List the things that are in your bucket right now!

2. Read 1 Peter 5:7-11

    - Write down a list of the ways God cares for you. Compare your two buckets. May your "Bucket of Grace" be overflowing with God's goodness!

3. Read Romans 8:37-39
   - Is there anything or anyone you have placed as more important than God? Take time to pray and offer this to God. Let nothing separate you from His love.

Group Discussion

1. Read Acts 9:1-9
   - What did Paul set out to do? Compare this to your intentions when you set out to do something that you know is not of God.

   - How did God get Paul's attention? What has God done in the past to get your attention?

   - Why would God have Paul be blinded for 3 days? Why do we get blinded at times?

- Look at verse 18, is there anything preventing you from seeing God's direction for your life?

2. Read Psalm 84:12
   - How are you trusting God with your family?

   - Describe your position when it comes to trusting God. What do you feel it will take to stay in a position of surrender?

TIMING IS EVERYTHING

Chapter 4

There is a time for everything, and a season for every activity under heaven.

— Ecclesiastes 3:1

Personal Reflection

1. Read Joshua 3:9-17
   - Describe the next step God is asking you to take. What are some small ways you can trust Him enough to take it?

2. Read 1 Kings 19:11-13
   - What are some ways that God tends to get your attention? How can you take steps to be more prepared to hear the small whispers from the Lord?

3. Read 1 John 2:15-17
   - How is your heart set on the things God desires for you? Do you see any distractions in your life that prevent you from living fully for these desires the Lord has for you?

 Group Discussion

1. Read Genesis 12:1-4
   - Discuss a time when God has shown you something that doesn't make sense, but you knew you needed to be obedient and follow Him. What was that like for you?

2. Read Isaiah 26:3
   - Remember, peace abounds with godly decisions. Talk about a time you had peace during a decision you needed to make.

FRIENDS... JUST THE RIGHT PEOPLE AT JUST THE RIGHT TIME

Chapter 5

Many people will walk in and out of your life, but only true friends will leave footprints in your heart.

— Eleanor Roosevelt

Personal Reflection

1. Read Proverbs 17:17
   - What can you do to be more Christ-like in your friendships? How will you show love at all times even in tough situations?

   - How do you display high moral character in and out of friendships?

   - How do you resemble someone of honor?

   - How are you generous with your time and resources?

- What needs to change so you can be more honorable in your friendships?

2. Read 1 Samuel 20:4, 23:16-17, and 2 Samuel 1:26
   - Can you think of someone who left footprints in your life? Were they footprints of joy or were they heavy embedded prints that stomped out your life?

   - Please share an experience you have had in friendship and what you truly desire out of future friendships.

Group Discussion

1. Read Proverbs 27:17
   - What looks different between someone who sharpens you and someone who doesn't? What qualities should you look for in a friendship that provides sharpening?

2. Read Ecclesiastes 3:1-14
   - One of the hardest things in friendships can be letting one go. Especially when there isn't an explanation for it.
   - How is it difficult for you to see friendships as a seasonal thing?
   - Can you share an example of a seasonal friendship you have experienced?
   - What other seasons of your life do you need to entrust to God? What steps will you take to entrust these seasons to the Lord?

VICTORY IN THE BATTLES

Chapter 6

It is impossible to win the race unless you venture to run, impossible to win the victory, unless you dare to battle.

— Richard M. Devos

 Personal Reflection

1. Read 1 Corinthians 9:24-27
   - What's keeping you from running the race well?

2. Read Hebrews 12:1-2
   - Remember there is One who ran the race before you. Fix your eyes on Him! Take a moment to pray in silence about the things you need to lay at the cross, so you can continue to run the race well!

3. Read Galatians 5:6-8
   - Is there someone or something that has cut you off from the path/race you were running?

- What do you need to do to follow God's voice and His guidance?

4. Read "Better than my Best" poem by Annie Johnson Flint on page 47.
   - How can you relate to Annie in this poem?

   - How do you struggle with control? In what ways can you surrender control to the Lord on a daily basis?

Group Discussion

1. Read 2 Corinthians 12:9
   - How have you seen God's power made perfect in your weakness?

2. Read Ephesians 1:4-8
   - For each phrase, write down what they mean to you and how you will apply them to your day-to-day life in the Lord?

   He chose you

   In love

   to be adopted

   glorious grace

   freely given

   we have redemption

   through His blood

   Lavished on us

DADDY, DADDY

Chapter 7

Father in Heaven! When the thought of thee wakes in our hearts, let it not awaken like a frightened bird that flies about in dismay, but like a child waking from sleep with a heavenly smile.

— Soren Kierkegaard

 Personal Reflection

1. Read Psalm 1:1-3
   - Are you like a tree planted by streams of water?

   - What kind of fruit do you pray your life will produce?

2. Read Isaiah 64:8
   - In what ways do you hold back from embracing this?

   - How can you relate with Madeleine L'Engle's quote on page 56 , first line?

- How will you choose to embrace the story God wants to write for your life?

3. Read Colossians 2:2-3
   - The mystery of God was made known through Christ. Among His treasures for you are wisdom and knowledge. Cherish the unknown days of your life because the One who knows you has great treasures stored up for each one of those days that lie ahead.

   - What joys do you anticipate as you read this passage?

Group Discussion

1. Read Psalm 37:4
   - What does it look like to delight yourself in the Lord?

   - Can you share a time when you delighted yourself in the Lord and He gave you the desires of your heart?

2. Read Matthew 6:25-34
   - What are the different ways you see your heavenly Father caring for you in this passage?

   - What are the ways He shows you your value in this passage?

   - How can you apply and live out this Truth?

3. Read Habakkuk 3:2
   - Can you share a time when God left you in awe?

TIME IS NOT OURS

Chapter 8

God has given me this day to use it as I will. I can waste it or use it for good, but what I do today is important, because I am exchanging a day of my life for it!

— Heartsill Wilson

 Personal Reflection

1. Read Psalm 84:10-11

   - Describe what you feel when you read this passage. What does it stir in your heart?

   - How can you change the way you live your day to better reflect a heart fixed on the things of Christ?

2. Read Philippians 4:4

   - Take time to memorize this verse. Then, every morning repeat it to yourself before you even open your eyes to face the day. See how different your life can be when you start your day in a joyful attitude. Remember, you can make the choice every day to live joyfully!

3. Read Psalm 43:4-5
   - David made a decision to put his hope in God. Will you make the same decision even when your heart is downcast?

   - How will you play music to the Lord? David played his harp, how will you worship God?

Group Discussion

1. Read 1 Chronicles 29:14-18
   - How are you spending your bank account?

   - Do you realize that your days here on earth are but a shadow compared to eternity? How will you spend each moment wisely?

2. Read Matthew 5:13
   - How will you add flavor to someone's life this week for God?

REFOCUSING THE VIEW

Chapter 9

Why did the achievers overcome problems while thousands are overwhelmed by theirs? They refused to hold on to the common excuses for failure. They turned their stumbling blocks into stepping stones. They realized that they couldn't determine every circumstance in life but they could determine their choice of attitude towards every circumstance.

— John C. Maxwell

Personal Reflection

1. Read Jeremiah 2:13
   - Have you ever tried to take care of something yourself and made a big mess of things? How could it have been different if you waited on God?

   - Remember, God size tasks are for God!

2. Read Psalm 51:10-12
   - What do you need to do to rid yourself of the distractions in your life, so you can "clear the mechanism" and be more focused?

3. Read Hebrews 11:1
   - How can you learn from the faith displayed in Noah, Abraham, Joseph, and Moses?

   - What is something you need to entrust to God right now?

Group Discussion

1. Read Matthew 5:6
   - What are some of the things that non-Christians hunger and thirst for in life?

   - In what ways can we satisfy our hunger and thirst in God?

2. Read 1 Kings 17:7-16
   - How did God meet the needs of the widow?

   - Can you share a time when God met your needs?

LIVING THE LIFE

Chapter 10

While we may not be called to martyr our lives, we must martyr our way of life. We must put our selfish ways to death and march to a different beat. Then the world will see Jesus.

— John C. Maxwell

Personal Reflection

1. Read the above quote.
   - Why must "we martyr our way of life?"

   - What does it look like when we do?

2. Read Hebrews 12:2
   - How does it make you feel to know that Christ embraced the cross for you?

3. Read Matthew 9:18-26
   - Jesus stopped for everyone who needed Him. Are there times when you are unwilling to stop? Why or why not?

Group Discussion

1. Read Matthew 28:18-20
   - Why do you think some of Jesus last words to us were "to go…?"

   - What can you do this week to make a difference in someone's life?

2. Read 1 John 3:18
   - What does it look like to carry out this verse?

   - In what practical ways can you show the love of Jesus this week?

AN EAGLE'S FLIGHT

Chapter 11

If I find in myself desires which nothing in this world can satisfy, the only logical explanation is that I was made for another world.

— C. S. Lewis

 Personal Reflection

1. Read Jeremiah 29:11
   - How does it make you feel to know this? Do you believe it?

2. Read Psalm 46:10
   - What does it look like to be still and listen?

   - Write down the desires that are on your heart right now and then look at the six questions at the end of the chapter. Look at each desire and compare them with the questions. Find out what desires are from God and what desires may not be God given

Group Discussion

1. Read James 4:13-17
   - This life is but a moment compared to the reality God is setting up for you in eternity. How does it make you feel to know that this world can't compare with what's to come?

2. Psalm 39:5
   - When you think about life on this earth being but a glimpse, how does it change the way you think?

   - How does it feel to know this life is "but a breath"?

3. Read Psalm 37:23-24
   - Can you share a time when God caught you? What did it feel like to fall into the hand of the Father?

FINDING TRUE NORTH

Chapter 12

Commit to the Lord whatever you do, and your plans will succeed.

— Proverbs 16:3

 Personal Reflection

1. Read Deuteronomy 6:4-9
   - If someone were to watch you for a week, to what would they say you are committed by the end of the seven-day period?

   - How does your life reflect a commitment to God or your own purpose?

2. Read Psalm 37:5
   - What are you committed to right now?

   - How do your commitments reflect that you have a relationship with Jesus?

3. Read Hebrews 12:1-2 & Philippians 3:12-14
   - Describe what commitment looks like in these scripture passages.

   - How do you need to change things to align yourself with God and His purpose for your life?

Group Discussion

1. Read Galatians 6:7-9
   - Describe what it looks like to sow to the sinful nature.

   - What does it look like to sow to please the Spirit?

2. Psalm 39:5
   Sow a thought and you reap an act;
   Sow an act and you reap a habit;
   Sow a habit and you reap a character;
   Sow a character and you reap a destiny.

   - Describe the kind of destiny you would like to reap with your life.

   - Describe the legacy you would like to leave.

PLAN OF ACTION

Chapter 13

The man who reads but one book, and that book His Bible, and then meditates much upon it, will be a better scholar in Christ's school than he who merely reads hundreds of books, and meditates not at all.

— Charles Spurgeon

 Personal Reflection

1. Read Romans 12:2
   - Take time to memorize this verse.
   - Develop your plan of action.
   - Meditate on the passage. Let it sink in.
   - Set a plan. What areas can you apply this scripture verse in your life?
   - Take action. Write down what it looks like to take action in your life regarding this verse.

2. Read 1 John 2:15-17
   - What are some of the ways you are conforming to this world?

3. Read Romans 8:37-39
   - Find Scripture to help you counteract the ways you have conformed to the world.
   - Remember, you are more than a conqueror and every day you will face a choice to conform to the world's patterns or to reflect the image of your Creator.

4. Read 1 Peter 1:3-9
   - Rejoice in the Living Hope you have in Jesus, as a child of God!
   - Describe how it feels to be so loved by God.
   - Describe a time you have felt God's love.

Group Discussion

1. Read Colossians 3:1-17
   - Please share a verse in this passage that impacts your life and explain why it impacts you so much.

- According to what you see in Colossians 3, what do you need to change to live more completely for God?

- What are some ways you can impact and influence the circle of people around you?

2. Read 1 John 4:7-12

    - How is God's love being made complete in your life?

LET'S TALK

Chapter 14

In prayer, it is better to have heart without words, than words without heart. Prayer will make a man cease from sin, or sin entice a man to cease from prayer. The spirit of prayer is more precious than treasures of gold and silver. Pray often, for prayer is a shield to the soul, a sacrifice to God, and a scourge for Satan.

— John Bunyan

 Personal Reflection

1. Read Philippians 4:6
   - Take the time to memorize this verse.
   - What are you anxious about right now? Will you trust God to take care of it?
   - "In everything" ~ In what ways will you choose to come to God in prayer?
   - "with thanksgiving" ~ How will you come to God with a heart of gratefulness when you pray?

2. Read Psalm 51:10
   - Please write down anything you need to confess to God.

   - Who do you need to forgive? How can you purify your heart before the Lord?

3. Read Luke 23:32-34
   - Jesus knew God and prayed like it.
   - Do you pray like you know God? If not, how will you change this?

   - Ask God to make Himself real to you, so you can experience something fresh in your prayer life.

Group Discussion

1. Read Psalm 86:5-13
   - Why is prayer essential to the Christian walk?

- What are the things David is asking for, declaring, and thanking God for?

- How does this prayer change the way you view prayer?

2. Read 2 Chronicles 7:14
   - What posture do we need to take when approaching God in prayer?

   - Can you share a prayer that God has answered in your life?

LETTING GOD SPEAK

Chapter 15

If you lower the ambient noise of your life and listen expectantly for those whispers of God, your ears will hear them. And when you follow their lead, your world will be rocked.

— Bill Hybels

 Personal Reflection

1. Read Psalm 119:9-16

   - How do your listening skills increase when you are in the Word more?

   - Describe a time you have experienced guidance from the Lord through His Word.

2. Read Romans 1:20

   - Describe a time when God's creation left you in awe and utterly speechless.

- Describe the last time God spoke to you through His creation and what it was like to hear Him in this way.

3. Read Matthew 6:25-34
   - Take time to read through this passage verse by verse and take note of how God has and is being faithful to you.

   - How does this passage challenge you?

   - What are some things you are worrying about that you need to hand over to God? Will you seek Him and His purpose for your life?

Group Discussion

1. Read 1 Kings 19:11-12
   - What are some ways that God speaks to you?

- Share a time when God has clearly spoken to you?

2. Read John 3:16-17
   - Share how God's love story has unfolded for you?

   - What was it that drew you into His love and what keeps you there?

STRETCH THOSE LEGS

Chapter 16

The more of God's Word you know and love, the more of God's Spirit you will experience.

— John Piper

 Personal Reflection

1. Read Exodus 3:7-15

   - Describe a time you tried to squirm your way out of something that God clearly asked you to do.

   - What do you think is the most important thing to remember from this passage of scripture? Hint: It's in verse14.

   - It doesn't matter what God asks of you, all that matters is that you know the power that you have when you are sent in Him!

2. Read Joshua 3:7-17

   - How does the crossing of the Jordan differ from the crossing of the Red Sea?

- Have you had times in your life when you have had to step in to the water before God performed a miracle in your life? What was that like?

3. Read Joshua 4:18-24
   - How has God used a miracle in your life?

   - Take time to meditate on verse 24 and ask God how you can be available for His work. What needs to change so you can experience the hand of God in your life?

Group Discussion

1. Read James 1:22-25
   - What steps will you take today to live out this passage of scripture?

- How has God challenged you lately by something in His Word?

2. Read 2 Corinthians 5:7
   - What did this mean in Moses time?

   - What does this mean in your life?

   - How does this Scripture back up your need for obedience in God even when things sound crazy?

Wearing the Right Shoe

Chapter 17

He is no fool who gives what he cannot keep to gain what he cannot lose.

— Jim Elliot

 Personal Reflection

1. Read Matthew 6:19-21

   - What do you think Jesus meant when He said this?

   - Define where your treasure is today and where you want it to be.

2. Read Isaiah 30:21

   - Describe a time you felt like you were walking in two different size shoes when it comes to this life. How did that feel? What was awkward about it?

   - It's important to distinguish the voice of the Father from the voice of the world.

- Ask the Lord to increase your ability to listen and pray for a great sensitivity to the guidance of His Holy Spirit.

3. Read Psalm 63:2-5

    God is most glorified in us when we are most satisfied in Him. — John Piper

    - On a scale of 1 to 10, how satisfied are you in God right now?

    - What are some things you can you do to become more satisfied in Him, so He can be more glorified in you?

Group Discussion

1. Read Psalm 37:6
    - In the book, I describe a picture of a rainbow, treasure hunts with my mom, and a treasure map from a movie. Describe what you see when you read this verse.

    - To further explore a life of righteousness read…

        Genesis 15:1-6
        Why was Abraham credited with righteousness?

Proverbs 21:21
How can you apply this verse to your life?

Matthew 5:6
What does it mean to hunger and thirst for righteousness?

Matthew 6:33
What does it look like to seek His righteousness?

A WALK THROUGH THE WOODS

Chapter 18

Never be afraid to trust an unknown future to a known God.

— Corrie Ten Boom

 Personal Reflection

1. Read Matthew 4:3-4
   - Even Jesus needed the Word of God. How much more do you need it?

   - Describe a time you felt lost in a spiritual forest or desert.

   - How did you depend on God's Word to get you through it?

2. Read Proverbs 3:5-6
   - Describe where your trust is.

- Define who or what you are relying on.

3. Read James 1:17
   - How does this make you feel knowing that God will not "change like shifting shadows?"

4. Read Hebrews 13:8
   - Do you believe this?
   - How has God proven this to be true in your life?

Group Discussion

1. Read the above quote from Corrie Ten Boom.
   - Describe your initial reaction to this quote.
   - What is God asking you to entrust to Him?

2. Read Matthew 4:10
   - The Word of God is powerful. "Away from me Satan!"

- Describe some times when you have pulled out the big guns on Satan and seen the power of God come through?

3. Read Hebrews 4:14-16
    - What does it mean to you that Jesus can sympathize with your weaknesses? How have you seen the Lord sympathize with you during a painful experience, dry time in life, or trial?

DELIGHTFUL VALUE

Chapter 19

The climax of God's happiness is the delight He takes in the echoes of His excellence in the praises of His people.

— John Piper

Personal Reflection

1. Read Luke 4:42, Matthew 14:23, and Luke 6:12
   - Do you truly understand and value the importance of time alone with God?

   - What can you do to make time with God a priority in your day?

2. Read John 12:3 & 7-8, and Mark 14:9
   - Do you have something in your life that holds high value and needs to be poured out before God?

   - How will you surrender your prized possessions to the King?

3. Read Matthew 19:16-24
   - At what cost will you follow Jesus completely?

   - Is there anything you are unwilling to give up? Why or why not?

   - How will you teach others the importance of making the right decision?

4. Read Matthew 6:33-34
   - Are you willing to say the following 3 things?

     I will seek first God's Kingdom!
     I will seek His righteousness!
     I will not worry about tomorrow!

   - Take time to make these 3 "I will's" a part of your every day. Write them out on a note card and reflect on them throughout your day. Describe the difference it has made to reflect on these three things.

Group Discussion

1. Read Psalm 37:4
   - Who is someone you enjoy delighting yourself around and why?

   - Is there someone who sees value inside of you and draws that out of you every time you're near them, like the times I was with my grandfather? What are the things they do to draw this out of you?

2. Read Zephaniah 3:17
   - How does it feel to know God takes great delight in you?

   - Can you share a time when you felt truly loved by God?

   - Rejoice together in the work of God and His love for you.

CALL TO COMMITMENT

Chapter 20

No horse gets anywhere until he is harnessed. No steam or gas ever drives anything until it is confined. No Niagara is ever turned into light and power until it is tunneled. No life ever grows great until it is focused, dedicated, disciplined.

— Harry Emerson Fosdick

 Personal Reflection

1. Read Matthew 26:36-46
   - How can you identify with the emotions that Jesus felt on His way to the cross?

   - Describe some action steps you will take to follow through on your commitment in prayer.

   - Are you willing to do what hurts for God?

2. Read Hebrews 11
   - God has and always will be faithful. If there was a new chapter written for men and women of faith, how would your name appear?

- How would you like it to appear?

- Describe what needs to change for you to see your name on the list?

Group Discussion

1. How does the quote from Harry Emerson Fosdick make sense in your life?

2. Read 2 Corinthians 10:3-6
   - Do you recognize the spiritual war you are in?

   - How have you experienced the war and what have you done to stand up against the enemy?

3. Read Ephesians 6:10-18
   - Are you ready for the spiritual battle that goes on 24/7?

   - What can you do to be prepared for the battle this week?

   - Why do you think it's important to walk ready in the full armor of God?

CALL TO COMMITMENT

Chapter 21

A chameleon lizard has the ability to change its color to blend into whatever atmosphere it is in. We are not to be 'chameleon Christians,' trying to blend in wherever we are, but are to be strikingly different.

— Author unknown

Personal Reflection

1. Read John 3:16 & 1 John 3:16

   - What was it like when you realized God loved you enough to send His Son Jesus to die in your place?

   - Describe that moment when you gave your life to Jesus and what your life has looked like since that moment in time.

2. Read Ephesians 2:8-9

   - How does it make you feel knowing that you can't earn your way to Heaven?

 ***Group Discussion***

1. Read Romans 3:23 & 6:23
   - Write down some people who you know need to hear the message of the cross. Pray that God will bring someone their way to share the Gospel with them or give you the courage to do it.

2. Read John 14:6
   - Take time to list and pray over those in your life who still have yet to know the redemptive work of Jesus Christ! Have you accepted God's free gift of eternal life? If not, here are 4 simple steps for you!

4 SIMPLE STEPS TO MAKE JESUS THE LORD OF YOUR LIFE

1. Admit that you are a sinner.

   There is no one righteous, not even one. —Romans 3:10

2. Be willing to turn from sin (repent).

   For the wages of sin is death, but the gift of God is eternal life in Christ Jesus our Lord. —Romans 6:23

3. Believe that Jesus Christ died for you, was buried, and rose from the dead.

   That if you confess with your mouth, "Jesus is Lord," and believe in your heart that God raised him from the dead, you will be saved. For it is with your heart that you believed and are justified, and it is with your mouth that you confess and are saved.

   —Romans 10:9-10

4. Through prayer, invite Jesus into your life to become your personal Savior.

   Everyone who calls on the name of the Lord will be saved.
   —Romans 10:13

Please pray this prayer, if you want to make Jesus the Lord of your life!

Dear Father God, I am a sinner and I need your forgiveness. I believe that Jesus Christ died for my sins. I am willing to turn from my sin. I now invite Christ to come into my heart and be my personal Savior. In Jesus Name, Amen

Tell someone if you decide to make Jesus the Lord of your life. Find someone who can disciple you and encourage you in your new walk with the Lord. Open up the Bible every day and find what God would want to say to you through it. Find a local church and get involved. I promise you are only beginning the ride of your lifetime.

Please contact us at hope@thepricelessjourney.org if you have given your life to the Lord. We would like to send you a gift and help disciple you in who God is calling to you to be for His Kingdom purpose.

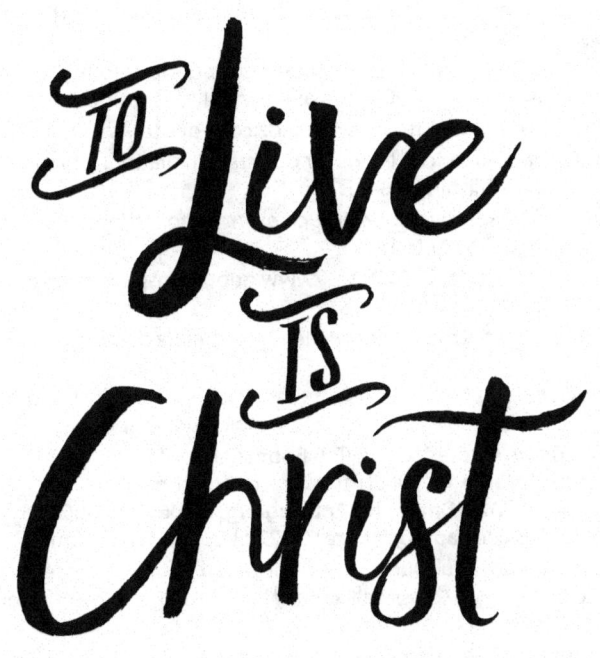

Bibliography

Author Unknown. 2006. <http://www.jesussite.com/quotes/righteousness.html.> Beers, Ronald, ed. Life Application Study Bible. Wheaton: Tyndale House Publishers, Inc. & Grand Rapids: Zondervan Publishing House, 1997.

Boom, Corrie Ten. 2006. <http://www.yourquotations.net/Corrie%20Ten%20Boom_quotes.html>.

Bunyan, John. 2006. <http://en.thinkexist.com/quotes/ john_bunyan/>. Christensen, James. 2006. <http:// www.alwaysbesideme.com/>.

DeVos, Richard. 2006. <http://www.zaadz.com/quotes/ view/30648>.

Dickens, Charles. American Notes for General Circulation. Whitefish: Kessinger Publishing, 1842.

Elliott, Jim. 2006. <http://www.intouch.org/myintouch/mighty/portraits/jim_Elliot_213678.html>.

Emerson, Ralph Waldo. 2006. http://www.quotationspage.com/quotes/Ralph_Waldo_Emerson/.

Chan, Francis. *Crazy Love: Overwhelmed by a Relentless God*. Colorado Springs: David C. Cook, 2008.

Christian Quotes. "223 Quotes About Grace." Accessed March 21, 2016. http://www.christianquotes.info/quotes-by-topic/quotes-about-grace/.

Corrie Ten Boom Quotes. "Corrie Ten Boom Quotes." Accessed March 13, 2016. http://l.facebook.com/l/TAQG4penPAQGQmKgXlwc2pDqugZug3KiT06hP9PmgG4n5_g/www.goodreads.com/author/quotes/102203.Corrie_ten_Boom.

Crosswalk. "40 Powerful Quotes from Corrie Ten Boom." Accessed March 21, 2016. http://www.crosswalk.com/faith/women/40-powerful-quotes-from-corrie-ten-boom.html.

Elliot, Elisabeth. *Keep a Quiet Heart*. Ann Arbor, MI: Vine Books, 1995.

Emerson, Ralph Waldo. 2006. http://www.quotationspage.com/quotes/Ralph_Waldo_Emerson/.

Evans, Darrell. "I Know." Freedom. Integrity, 2002.

Flint, Annie Johnson. 2006. <http://www.blessedquietness. com/journal/homemake/ajf-better.htm>.

———. 2006. <http://www.preceptaustin.org/annie_johnson_ flint's_ biography. htm>.

For Love of the Game. Dir. Sam Raimi. Perf. Kevin Costner and Kelly Preston. 1999. DVD. Universal Studios, 2000.

Fosdick, Harry. 2006. <http://www.quoteworld.org/quotes/4872>.

Foster, Richard. Celebration of Discipline. London: Hodder & Stoughton Religious Books, 1998.

Heartsill, Wilson. 2006. <http://www.jesussite.com/quotes/time.htm>.

Henry, Matthew. Matthew Henry's Commentary. Peabody: Hendrickson Publishers, Inc. 1991.

Kierkegaard, Soren. 2006. <http://www.quotesandpoem.com/quotes/listquotes/author/Soren_Kierkegaard>.

L'Engle, Madeleine. Excerpt from the poem "Act III, Scene II." 2006. <http://emp.byui.edu/Wad/honors221/poetic/act3.htm>.

Lewis, C.S. Mere Christianity. New York: Macmillan Publishing Co., Inc., 1977.
Maxwell, John C. 2006.<http://www.jesussite.com/quotes/attitude. htm>.

Moore, Waylon B. 2006. <http://www.mentoring-disciples.org/Quotes.html>.
Myers, G.A. Hugs for Friends book 2. West Monroe: Howard Publishing, 2003.

Piper, John. Desiring God—Meditations for a Christian Hedonist. Sisters: Multnomah Publishers, Inc. 2003.

Pursifull, Joe. 2006. <http://www.jesussite.com/quotes/grace.htm>. Reade, Charles. 2006. <http://quotes.zaadz.com/Charles_Reade>.

Roosevelt, Eleanor. 2006. <http://www.mtariders.com/memorials/>.

Spafford, Horatio. "It Is Well with My Soul." The Big Book of Hymns. Milwaukee: Hal Leonard Corporation, 1873.

Spurgeon, Charles. Excerpt from Meditation. 2006. <http://www.the-highway. com/meditation_Spurgeon.html>.

Tait, Michael. Jesus Freaks: Martyrs. 2006. <http://www.jesussite.com/quotes/living.htm>.

Tozer, A.W. The Attributes of God. Camp Hill: Christian Publications, 1997.
Worthen, Drew. Excerpt from sermon "Be Transformed By The Renewing Of Your Mind." 2006. <http://www.cyberstreet.com/calvary/rm12–2.htm>.

Wimber, John. Excerpt from Equipping the Saints Article. 1991. <http://www.vineyardusa.org/upload/Equipping%20the%20Saints.pdf>.

About the Author

To learn more about Sarah please visit thepricelessjourney.org

Also, find Sarah at:
>**Facebook:** https://www.facebook.com/thepricelessjourneyinc
>**Instagram:** pricelessjourney

You can also enjoy more of Sarah's books to help you in your walk with the Lord.

>***You Are Priceless***
>***Joyful Living***
>***Praying through the Gospels***
>***Victorious Mindset***
>***Wisdom for Life***
>***Clinging to God's Promises***
>***His Hope for your Destiny***
>***Make Your Moments Count***

www.ingramcontent.com/pod-product-compliance
Lightning Source LLC
Chambersburg PA
CBHW052055110526
44591CB00013B/2215